# All my ROOMS

By
Angie Wagler

The Transformation Series
Workbook Edition
—Volume 1—

# The Transformation Series – Volume 1

# All my ROOMS

Bringing transformation to the heart of where we live...

# ANGIE WAGLER

# The Workbook Edition

© Copyright 2016 – Angie Wagler
The Transformation Series Workbook Edition
Volume 1
Edition 1
All rights reserved.

This book may not be copied or reprinted for commercial gain or profit.
Scripture quotations are from the New International Version of the Bible,
unless otherwise indicated.

Cover & Book Design by Angie Wagler
Editing Team: Don Boyd, Angie Wagler

ISBN-13: 978-1530196821
ISBN-10: 1530196825

# ENDORSEMENTS

Angie Wagler's book *All My Rooms* is a delightfully practical look at life. By comparing a room of your house to a part of your life, she enables you to invite Jesus in and assist you in every way.

The Living Room correlates to our thought processes. The Family Room speaks of relationships, and how to forgive. From The Bedroom: "To sleep well, we need to put fear in its place!" Her personal story of doing this is greatly encouraging.

At the end of each chapter, Angie invites us to take some time to write down our own reaction to her teaching. This engaging book is one you will want to use over and over. Even as we sometimes move from place to place physically and need to "redecorate," at times, we also have to move in our thinking. *All My Rooms* gives a refreshing way for a spiritual spring cleaning and refocusing of our lives.

—*Jane Huff, Author, An Intimate Look at the Armor of God: Finding Safety in a Broken World*

*All My Rooms,* is insightful, inspiring and deep. Walking through 'my rooms' using this resource brought truth and life to me as I examined who I am, how God sees me, and received His love and truth to a greater measure.

Room by room, one by one, I invited God to come in—His presence was and is very powerful and life changing.

Thank you Angie, for this inspirational life changing gift.

*—Mary Wagler*

Angie is spiritually insightful as she compares the rooms of our home to the house of our souls. She takes us on a journey to explore the various activities and purposes of each room, and then asks us to look into our hearts to see what God says about that in our own lives.

I came to realize that every room—the kitchen, living room, family room, bedroom, bathroom and home office—has a purpose with a spiritual parallel. Most of the rooms in my "house" have areas that need work. For example, the living room in my home is the "good room", where we try to keep it clean and tidy at all times. It also doubles as the worship centre in my home, because the piano and guitars are kept there. As I prayed about my "living room", I felt God say that I don't go there nearly often enough. He wants me to spend time out with Him, worshiping Him everyday. He longs to have me draw nearer to Him more often.

I love the way Angie brings out these truths without making anyone feel like a failure. Her transparent sharing allows all of us to let down our guard and be real. She teaches people how to hear God speaking to them, and that is so refreshing!

*—Denise Bender*

# THIS BOOK IS
# DEDICATED TO:

### *My dear friend, Katie Foster*

This book is in existence because of you! I have been honoured to walk with you and witness the power of God at work, transforming you into His masterpiece. You are a "first-fruits" of what is coming. May the blossoms that have come forth in your life continue to grow into fruit that will remain.

### *The ladies of Living Water Community Christian Fellowship*

What a delightful bunch of ladies you are! I trust that, as you continue in your walk with Jesus, you will grow in wisdom and understanding, in your love for Him and others, and that you will cultivate time with Him, making room for Him in all the rooms of your house!

### *And last but not least, my husband, Paul*

You have been my greatest supporter. Whether I am awake or not, I know that you bless me early every morning to be all that I am destined to be. I love doing life with you!

# TABLE OF **CONTENTS**

Preface..................................................13

Introduction..........................................17

Chapter 1 - The House.............................................21
    House in the Bible – 22 – Trouble in the Temple – 24 – Foundations – 28 – Agreement – 29 – Jesus in My House – 31 – Invitation – 32 – Write it Down – 33

Chapter 2 - The Living Room................................39
    The Mind – 41 – Not Every Thought is Your Own – 42 – Temptation – 45 – Renewing the Mind – 46 – Through the Ceiling – 47 – Jesus in My Living Room – 48 – Invitation – 50 – Write it Down – 51

## Chapter 3 - The Family Room.................................57

Relationships – 58 – God is a Father – 61 – Forgiveness is a Choice – 64 – The "How To' – 69 – Jesus in My Family Room – 70 – Invitation – 70 – Write it Down – 71

## Chapter 4 - The Kitchen.................................79

The Heart – 81 – Appetite – 83 – Mastery – 86 – Are you Hungry? – 91 – Jesus in My Kitchen – 93 – Invitation – 94 – Write it Down – 95

## Chapter 5 - The Bedroom.................................101

Sleep – 102 – Worry an Enemy of Rest – 103 – Putting Fear in its Place – 105 – Peace and Rest – 107 – Dream – 109 – Intimacy - The Bride and the Bridegroom – 111 – Jesus in My Bedroom – 113 – Invitation – 113 – Write it Down – 114

## Chapter 6 - The Den.................................121

Secrets – 122 – Reflection – 124 – Repent – 125 – Shake off the Doldrums – 126 – God has Secrets – 128 – Jesus in My Den – 130 – Invitation – 130 – Write it Down – 131

## Chapter 7 - The Home Office.................................137

Stewardship and the Art of Managing – 139 – Called to Increase – 141 – Perspective – 145 – Exercise Your Faith Muscle – 147 – Jesus in My Home Office – 149 – Invitation – 150– Write it Down – 151

## Chapter 8 - The Garage...............................157

Storage – 158 – Understanding – 159 – Your Experiences – 161 – Your Testimony – 162 – Go – 165 – Jesus in My Garage – 166 – Invitation – 166 – Write it Down – 167

## Chapter 9 - The Bathroom...............................173

Perception – 174 – How does God See Us? – 176 – Flushing – 179 – Shower – 182 – Jesus in My Bathroom – 184 – Invitation – 184 – Write it Down – 185

## Conclusion...............................191

## More About Angie & Paul Wagler...............................193

## Other Books Available...............................195

## One Last Thing...............................199

# PREFACE

*Here I am! I stand at the door and knock.
If anyone hears my voice and opens the door,
I will come in and eat with that person,
and they with me.
Revelation 3:20*

The image in Revelation 3, where Jesus is at the door, knocking, is one that is both comforting and sobering. Comforting—because Jesus comes and knocks at our door, wanting to come in and sup with us. Sobering—because in this passage, He is knocking at the door of the church; hmmm, isn't He supposed to be on the inside? If we have invited Him in—to be Lord of our lives, why is He on the outside knocking?

Recently I was invited to speak at a church's women's retreat. The topic was up to me—so I did some fasting and praying and was given a word for them and some instruction as to what to teach, train and equip. I share with you below part of the word.

> "I love these ladies. They are my handiwork. I have called them—each one.
>
> I have called them to arise to grow in love and understanding, in their love for Me and others, in their understanding of My heart and My desire for them and those around them.
>
> They are precious to Me. I hold them in My hand. For surely, even as a painter paints or a puzzle is put together—each piece, each stroke is meant to be part of a glorious masterpiece.
>
> Even the sorrows, I weave into good. I call these ladies, "Mine."
>
> I desire them to grow in wisdom and stature before men and before Me.
>
> Teach them, train them, equip them to hear Me, to hear My voice, and to walk with Me.
>
> For I desire to meet them in all areas of their life—in their Living Room, Family Room, Kitchen, Bedroom, Den, Office, Garage, and even in the Bathroom.
>
> In each room, make room, for I come to meet with you.
>
> I come to meet with you."

This word, I believe, is not just for this group of ladies; I am convinced it is for all women, and for men, called by the Lord. The invitation is to go deeper in hearing Him and walking with Him in every area of life—the call to intimacy with God.

So, in this book, we are going to look at how to make room for Jesus in our lives. And, as in this word, we are going to look at the rooms of a house and see how they apply to us as individuals. From this vantage point, we can learn what Jesus may want to say and show to us in order to bring His transforming power into each room in our lives.

In this Workbook Edition, you will find wide margins—perfect to jot down any thoughts you may have while you are reading. As well, at the end of each chapter there is a reflective *Invitation* section, followed by a *Write it Down* section. The latter section includes a number of pages where you can literally *write it down*—record what you are hearing, seeing, and experiencing with Jesus. I encourage you to make use of this resource for later reflection and implementation of these new thoughts and revelations.

# INTRODUCTION

When I first got this word, my mind went in quite a number of directions about what to say and how to organize this topic. It felt overwhelming and exciting at the same time. How would I portray the concepts of this visitation in our rooms? I am very visual and like to have illustrations and items to drive home the points—to help with the understanding process.

My mind immediately went to a doll house. I loved playing with dolls when I was a child; baby dolls, Barbie dolls and Dawn dolls. (That will probably date me, but these "Dawn dolls" were much smaller than Barbie dolls; could travel well; and there was one named Angie that both my sister and I had. Any doll with the name "Angie" had to be the perfect doll for a child with the same name!)

I loved playing with my Barbie dolls too. I made a doll house out of cardboard boxes and spent many hours playing with it. My cousins had a real Barbie house with 3 or 4 floors and an elevator. It was certainly grander than my cardboard box house but imagination in a child is huge, so it was not an obstacle that caused much trouble for me.

I loved those experiences so much that I made a cardboard box doll house for my daughters when they were young. Five—or was it six? boxes all uniform sizing, windows made with plastic cut from old laundry baskets, real small scale wallpaper pasted on the walls, fabric for rugs, and curtains on the windows. It was much grander than the one I made as a girl.

It makes me smile thinking back to the kitchen, dining room, living room, bedrooms, and even bathroom. Yes, we even had a toilet in that house. Amazing what doll furniture is available!

So in thinking of my experiences with doll houses, I imagined that, for my sessions, I would have a doll house of some sort. As I would speak on each room, I would put a doll (of me) in it and then one of Jesus. What would He say? What would He reveal? What would He have me learn?

With this imagery in mind, each of us is a house with many rooms. Come with me on this journey of discovery to find out what Jesus wants us to learn as we tour our rooms. Will we find that we can, indeed, make room for Him in each of our rooms—in our whole house?

# Chapter 1

# THE HOUSE

*Unless the Lord builds the house,*
*the builders labor in vain.*
*—Solomon... Psalm 127:1*

I would be remiss if I did not begin this book with a chapter on the whole house. Now I know you might not live in a house. You might live in a condo, an apartment, a duplex, a cottage, or even a trailer—like I did when I was first married. But bear with me, the house is the image we are going with.

I am a house. You are a house. A house is a private establishment. It is not a public building. You don't just walk up and walk in—unless you know the owners well. You knock to gain access. There are certain boundaries and laws of the land, rules, if you will, to protect those who reside in the house and those who own the property.

If we are likening ourselves to a house, let's get some Biblical backup—some understanding on what this looks like from that perspective.

## HOUSE IN THE BIBLE

The word "house" is mentioned almost 2000 times in the Bible. Beginning with Genesis 7:1, where Noah was told to go into the ark,

> Then the Lord said to Noah, "Go into the ark, you and all your household, for I have seen that you are righteous before me in this generation."

and in Genesis 12:1 where Abram is given instruction of the Lord to

> ..."Go from your country and your kindred and your father's house to the land that I will show you."

The many references to "house" and "household," refer to the house, as not just a building where you reside, but to the family structure as well. You are born into your father's house, and the clan or tribe to which you belonged was also a house. The whole nation of Israel was referred to as a house. So was the church in the New Covenant. As it says in

1 Peter 2:5,

> …you yourselves, like living stones, are being built up as a spiritual house, to be a holy priesthood, to offer spiritual sacrifices acceptable to God through Jesus Christ.

The temple in the Old Testament scriptures was also called God's house. It was where He actually dwelled on Earth, with His presence above the mercy seat. (Ex 25:22) When Solomon dedicated the temple, the glory of the Lord filled it. In the New Covenant, we understand that, now, we are the temple where God dwells, both in a corporate sense and individually.

1 Corinthians 3:16

> Do you not know that you are God's temple and that God's Spirit dwells in you?

And 2 Corinthians 5:1 refers to our bodies as our home, our tent

> For we know that if the tent that is our earthly home is destroyed, we have a building from God, a house not made with hands, eternal in the heavens.

So we can safely say that we are, indeed, a house. And if we are believers and followers of Jesus, we are, in fact, a house where the Spirit of God has taken up residence.

That, My Friends, is a truth that we are to take hold of! The Holy Spirit lives in us! Each one of us!

## TROUBLE IN THE TEMPLE

Even as the presence of God was in the temple, and before that, the tabernacle in the wilderness, (and in the cloud by day and fire by night…but that is another thought for another day)…we'll stick with the temple and tabernacle for now.

Just as God's presence was in the temple and tabernacle, there were some situations that arose in the temple, that were not in keeping with the reality of His presence.

I am thinking about Eli—the high priest that we remember from the stories of Samuel, who, as a child, was taken to the tabernacle to live. Remember the story of Samuel? How he heard someone calling his name. Three times he ran to Eli, wondering what he wanted. On the third time, Eli realized that God was speaking to the child and instructed Samuel to say, 'Speak Lord, your servant is listening.'

In that first encounter Samuel had with hearing the Lord, he was actually given a rebuke to give to Eli—for the mismanagement of his house and for allowing his sons to continue to sin in the Tabernacle. Ouch!!! We don't often remember that part of the story!

Then there are accounts of how the temple fell into disarray and needed repair in the time of King Joash, and how repairs needed to be made in the time of King Josiah.

It is interesting to note that both these kings became king when they were children. During their reigns they fixed up the things that were falling apart. Didn't Jesus say, "...a child will lead them"? Well, they actually weren't kids anymore when they made the repairs, but something about what was instilled in the heart of a child would blossom in their adult years.

In the repairs that were happening under Josiah, a scroll of the Law was found in the temple. When it was read, they realized that the king, the priests and the people were not following God's law. King Josiah implemented reform to bring the country back under the blessing of God.

Ezekiel was taken in a vision, to see all the corruption

in the temple; and he saw the glory of God depart.

And the list goes on, if you care to research it. But why mention this?

We need to understand that we are given the Holy Spirit as a seal of our inheritance. We are daughters and sons of God. There are promises we are to inherit, just as the children of Israel had promises—to be taken into the Promised Land and promises to be blessed. Deuteronomy 28 is a great chapter that spells out both the blessings and the curses. We will look at the blessings below:

> If you fully obey the Lord your God and carefully follow all his commands I give you today, the Lord your God will set you high above all the nations on earth. 2 All these blessings will come on you and accompany you if you obey the Lord your God:
>
> 3 You will be blessed in the city and blessed in the country.
>
> 4 The fruit of your womb will be blessed, and the crops of your land and the young of your livestock—the calves of your herds and the lambs of your flocks.
>
> 5 Your basket and your kneading trough will be blessed.

6 You will be blessed when you come in and blessed when you go out.

7 The Lord will grant that the enemies who rise up against you will be defeated before you. They will come at you from one direction but flee from you in seven.

8 The Lord will send a blessing on your barns and on everything you put your hand to. The Lord your God will bless you in the land he is giving you.

9 The Lord will establish you as his holy people, as he promised you on oath, if you keep the commands of the Lord your God and walk in obedience to him.

10 Then all the peoples on earth will see that you are called by the name of the Lord, and they will fear you.

11 The Lord will grant you abundant prosperity—in the fruit of your womb, the young of your livestock and the crops of your ground—in the land he swore to your ancestors to give you.

12 The Lord will open the heavens, the storehouse of his bounty, to send rain on your land in season and to bless all the work of your hands. You will lend to many nations but will borrow from none.

13 The Lord will make you the head, not the tail. If you pay attention to the commands of the Lord your God

that I give you this day and carefully follow them, you will always be at the top, never at the bottom.

14 Do not turn aside from any of the commands I give you today, to the right or to the left, following other gods and serving them.

This is quite a thorough list! Do you know that these are your promises too?

## FOUNDATIONS

In the early 1990's, my husband, Paul, and I had the opportunity to build a house. Being the designer type person I am, I thought about it, dreamed about it, put my thoughts on paper, reworked it, dreamed some more, made more changes, and then we had the blueprints drawn up.

After that, the house was built. Yes, there was some revamping and things arose that needed attention; but, overall, the house looked like we envisioned…it was built based on the blueprints, on the plan that had been laid out.

Do you know that God has a dream for you—a plan for you? He has placed dreams and desires in you that are in keeping with who He has made you to be. There is a blueprint of what He has made you to look like, both in the physical reality and the spiritual.

It took a process, for our blueprint to become our house. We needed to hire a contractor and needed to commit to the process. A huge hole needed to be dug; truckloads of cement needed to go into the footings and the foundation before the structure could be built. And, once the structure went up, rooms were formed; and in went the materials to make the walls, floors, roof, etc. etc. It took time. I believe it was almost 6 months from the time we dug until we moved in—a process.

There is a blueprint for your life. It does not originate with you. It is from the heart of your Father God. He wants to build you into something beautiful and unique. There are gifts and abilities He has given you that the world will not see unless you release them in your unique way. You are unique. No one else has your voice, your sound, your viewpoints, your fingerprints.

## AGREEMENT

For those plans to be realized in your life, there needs to be something called 'agreement'. Have you understood that, when Jesus was tempted by the devil, the devil was after something? He wanted Jesus to agree with him.

'Oh Jesus you've been fasting. You're hungry. Hey, if you are the Son of God make this stone bread. See all these kingdoms of the world. They're mine, but I will give them to you, if you bow down and worship me. If you really are the Son of God, throw yourself down off this tower, because God will send his angels so your foot won't strike a stone!'

Jesus chose not to agree with his enemy. He chose, instead, to agree with His Father, His Father's heart, and His Father's mission for Him.

In this house journey, you will have some choices to make too. With whom will you agree?

Jesus has some good words to ponder, found in Matthew 7:24-27

> 24 "Everyone then who hears these words of mine and does them will be like a wise man who built his house on the rock. 25 And the rain fell, and the floods came, and the winds blew and beat on that house, but it did not fall, because it had been founded on the rock. 26 And everyone who hears these words of mine and does not do them will be like a foolish man who built his house on the sand. 27 And the rain fell, and the floods came, and the winds blew and beat against that house, and it fell, and great was the fall of it."

## JESUS IN MY HOUSE

This is the reflective time of our journey. We will have these sections at the end of each chapter. This is the time we will invite Jesus to come into each of our rooms, to talk with us, and to show us things about ourselves and others.

John 10:4 tells us that His sheep know His voice. But we will read a little more to give us a little more context. Jesus is talking about Himself as being the shepherd of the sheep.

> 2 The one who enters by the gate is the shepherd of the sheep. 3 The gatekeeper opens the gate for him, and the sheep listen to his voice. He calls his own sheep by name and leads them out.
>
> 4 When he has brought out all his own, he goes on ahead of them, and his sheep follow him because they know his voice.
>
> 5 But they will never follow a stranger; in fact, they will run away from him because they do not recognize a stranger's voice."

If you are new in this journey, you, too, will hear His voice. It may come as a faint thought, a picture, some understanding, or just a knowing. Just go with it. There will be some statements and questions to guide you through this time.

Quiet yourself and have a pencil or pen handy to jot down what you experience. Your experience with the Lord is important. What He speaks to your heart is valuable.

> ## INVITATION:
>
> Invite Jesus to come into your house.
>
> - Jesus, I understand that You're knocking at my door.
>
> - I want You to come in and talk with me.
>
> - I want You to show me how You see me.
>
> - Show me what You have put within me that needs to be awakened.
>
> - Show me if there are areas and things I need to break my agreement with.

# WRITE IT DOWN...

# Chapter 2

# THE **LIVING** ROOM

*If then you have been raised with Christ, seek the things that are above, where Christ is, seated at the right hand of God. Set your minds on things that are above, not on things that are on earth. For you have died, and your life is hidden with Christ in God.*
*Colossians 3:1-3*

The Living Room is the room in which you live! Now that may not always be the case. In our first home—the trailer—we did do a lot of living in our living room. Our trailer looked like a little bungalow and had been moved onto the family farm in two pieces, split down the middle and then reattached. It had no basement and was set on cement pillars that had been poured in the ground. It had three small bedrooms, a bathroom, laundry room, storage room, kitchen, dining room, and living room. And, yes, we did do a lot of living in that room.

Our second home, the house we built, had both a living room and family room on the main floor. For the duration of our five plus years there, we had no living room furniture! The living room was, in essence, the children's playroom, filled with toys, a child-size table and chairs, and a little cupboard unit, made by Paul's brother, that housed all sorts of children's dishes and play food.

The home in which we live now does have a living room with furniture! I was not going to go without when we moved into our delightful old Tudor style house.

How do you use your living room? What do you like about it? Is it the colour of the walls, the softness of your sofa, or the pictures on the wall?

The females in our family spend a lot of time in the living room, reading, visiting and relaxing. It is where the dog has her perch on the sofa to look out the front window, watching the goings on up and down the street—what every good watch dog does! It is the room where I get my guitar out to play and worship, the room where we have tea and goodies with friends, and the room where we can nap if we find that is necessary.

## THE MIND

I used to like to listen to Bob Jones, the prophet from the States, who passed away on Valentine's Day, 2014. He had such a unique way of talking—metaphoric and 'in parables'. He, often, would refer to the mind as our living room.

How true, our thoughts create our reality. What does it look like if Jesus is knocking at our Living Room door? Knocking at our mind's door? Wanting to have a little chat with us about how we think? What we think? What we think about?

Isaiah 55:8-9 are verses the Lord has taken me to time and time again

> 'For my thoughts are not your thoughts, neither are your ways my ways,' declares the LORD.

> 'For as the heavens are higher than the earth, so are my ways higher than your ways and my thoughts than your thoughts.'

I *think* that we sometimes *think* that what we are *thinking* is what God also *thinks*. Not necessarily true, as the Lord has reminded me on a number of occasions.

He desires to relate with us and share His thoughts with us so we can get to know Him better and so that we also can become more like Him. It comes back again to our agreement.

When the devil tempted Jesus, how did he word things? He used Scripture—the very Word of God to tempt Jesus! How did Jesus battle? He used Scripture too! This time of testing came at the end of Jesus' 40 days of fasting and praying and being tempted in the wilderness.

But Jesus had the presence of mind and the understanding to know what was in the Father's heart, to battle and to agree with the Father's plan for Him.

## NOT EVERY THOUGHT IS YOUR OWN

When I was young, my mother read us, her children, Bible stories from a multiple volume set of illustrated books. I still vividly remember the picture, from those books, of the devil tempting Jesus. He was cunning looking, dark, evil, and looked like a very bad angel indeed!

And no doubt he does. But he is also a liar, a deceiver, and a masquerader. When the devil, Satan, Lucifer, Beelzebub, the accuser, the angel of light, the prince of the air, or whatever name he may be called at any given time, comes to tempt us—how does he come?

Often he comes with or as a thought. I am not saying he only comes one way; that is way too simplistic! It is a whole lot easier to say, "No," to the devil when we recognize it's him than if we think it's us.

We need to recognize that not all our thoughts are our own. A good deal of them are our own; however the enemy can also tempt us through our thoughts and God also can speak to us through them.

2 Corinthians 10:5

> We demolish arguments and every pretension that sets itself up against the knowledge of God, and we take captive every thought to make it obedient to Christ.

This verse points out that we have something to do regarding our thoughts. We test our thoughts to see if they are in line with God's truth in Jesus. If not, they have to be taken captive. What imagery! Can you picture it? How would you take a thought captive?

Would you come, riding in on a horse, with your cowboy hat on, and lasso that damaging thought, tying it up tight? Or would you come in with your guns drawn and raised like a detective, moving in from doorframe to doorframe, peeking around corners, until there's a gun battle and you take down the enemy?!!

It does seem a little funny to talk about taking a thought—a thought from your mind, or a thought from my mind—captive in this way. But we need to understand that the biggest battle goes on in the minds of humanity. As followers of Jesus, we are not excluded from this battle. It actually intensifies, because of the hope to which we are called. Because we carry, in our DNA as a new creation, the plans and purposes of God which are yet to be accomplished on the Earth.

Yes, I will say it again in another way. We partner with God to bring about His kingdom purpose here, on the planet. It does get the devil rather concerned when we recognize our call and walk in the power and anointing available to us.

The apostle Paul, in 2 Corinthians 2:11, tells us that we are not unaware of the devil's schemes. There are things for us do so Satan will not outwit us.

He's a schemer; has a plan to mess you up, to derail you from God's plan for you; and he wants to use you to do it. How? Through the power of your agreement.

## TEMPTATION

Let's look at temptation. It starts with a thought.

James 1:13-14

> When tempted, no one should say, "God is tempting me." For God cannot be tempted by evil, nor does he tempt anyone; but each person is tempted when they are dragged away by their own evil desire and enticed.

Ouch! There is a thing with temptation. There needs to be hook—something that seems desirable. Something we want. There are some sins people get caught up in that I probably never would, simply because I have no desire for them. And the reverse would also be true. I would be more susceptible to getting derailed in certain circumstances than others, based on who I am, how I see things, and what my desires are.

Did you notice, when we talked about Jesus being tempted, that He was tempted with some of the very things for which He was destined? Yes, He was tempted to get them without the cost by switching allegiance.

Sometimes, it is the very thing in our destiny that can catch us up. Take Moses for instance, called to be a deliverer. God had made him in way to be compatible with that call. He had a strong sense of injustice; so much so that he took matters in his own hands, before his time, and killed an Egyptian taskmaster who had been mistreating a Hebrew slave.

Psalm 37:4 tells us

> Delight yourself in the Lord and He will give you the desires of your heart.

There are desires that God has put in you. If we agree with Heaven, they are fulfilled for good in our lives. If we agree with the enemy, we are set up for some troubling times. He has a way of taking a foot when you give an inch.

## RENEWING THE MIND

In Romans 12:2 we are told

> Do not be conformed to this world, but be transformed by the renewal of your mind, that by testing you may discern what is the will of God, what is good and acceptable and perfect.

Our minds need to be transformed. We do this by talking control of our thoughts—evaluating them and discerning them. This means disagreeing with those things that are not in keeping with the thoughts and heart of God and purposely thinking in a way that is consistent with God's thinking towards us and others.

Philippians 4:8 tells us

> 8 Finally, brothers and sisters, whatever is true, whatever is noble, whatever is right, whatever is pure, whatever is lovely, whatever is admirable—if anything is excellent or praiseworthy—think about such things.

And in Colossians 3:17, we are reminded to give thanks in all we say and do.

> And whatever you do, whether in word or deed, do it all in the name of the Lord Jesus, giving thanks to God the Father through him.

## THROUGH THE CEILING

Recently, some friends of ours, Sheldon and Judy, had an issue with a water leak making a mark on their living room ceiling. Wanting to figure it out, Sheldon maneuvered himself up into the crawl space of their attic to have a look at what was going on up there. Before he went up, Judy was uneasy. She voiced her concern, that she was afraid he wouldn't be careful enough and put his foot through the ceiling. Sheldon thought her fears unfounded, until he shifted his position and did, indeed, put his foot through the ceiling, making a hole and a mess that needed fixing, besides the other issues that needed to be addressed.

Judy was rather livid, but I believe she has since settled down. When they started to share the story with me, I immediately knew there was a prophetic message in it.

The word for them is also for you and me. God wants to take us higher. There will be a hole punched in our living room ceilings—our minds, our understanding. New ideas from the heart of God will expand our understanding to shift us into new things—new ways of doing things, and new understandings of how things work. It may be uncomfortable, make a bit of a mess, and need some reconstruction: but get ready and make room for some divine thoughts coming your way that will bring change.

## JESUS IN MY LIVING ROOM

So we have equated our living room to our mind—to how we think. It is time to invite Jesus into your living room.

I encourage you to quiet yourself. Lay down on your living room couch, if you so desire. Close your eyes, if you wish. Have a pen or pencil handy. You will want to record what you see, hear or experience. You can do that in the *Write it Down* section at the end of the chapter.

As Habakkuk 2:2 says

> Then the Lord answered me and said, "Write the vision And engrave it plainly on [clay] tablets So that the one who reads it will run. AMP

I have found it very helpful to write down what God has shown me or spoken to me. If I do not write it down, I will forget portions, or all, of what was spoken. To the degree you are faithful to steward what He reveals, will determine how you grow in your ability to hear, discern and walk in kingdom ways.

God will speak to us in different ways. He may speak so that you actually hear words in your mind or even audibly. He may give you a picture in your mind's eye, or a song may come to mind. You might have a vision or just a faint impression. You may not hear anything, or you may just feel an emotion such as peace. Go with it. Below are some things you can ask to help you guide this time.

## INVITATION:

Invite Jesus to come:

- Jesus, I thank You that You want to come and meet with me in all my rooms.

- I invite You to come.

- Show me my Living Room.

- How do You see me?

- What do You want to show me?

- What do I believe that You want me to see differently?

- How does my thinking need to change to line up with Your thoughts?

- What are Your thoughts towards me?

- Show me how I can agree with You in order for Your purposes to be fulfilled in my life?

# WRITE IT DOWN...

# CHAPTER 2 — THE LIVING ROOM

# CHAPTER 2 — THE LIVING ROOM

# Chapter 3

# THE **FAMILY** ROOM

*Anyone who loves their brother and sister lives in the light, and there is nothing in them to make them stumble.*
*1 John 2:10*

Do you have a family room? Sometimes, the living room and family room are, in essence, the same room. In the last number of years, the 'Great Room' had been edging the family room out in popularity. After all, who wouldn't want to spend time in a great room?

When I was growing up, the common name for this type of room was the 'Rec Room'—short for 'Recreation Room.' When I was young, I thought it was the 'Wreck

Room'. I guess that sometimes it must have looked that way, as it was the room with the cable TV and all our toys!

Do you spend a lot of time in your family room? Ours is in the basement with our reclining sectional and TV mounted above the fireplace. Someone in the house (that would be my husband), loves sports. There can be a lot of sports playing on the television, especially in winter. After all, we are Canadians! We also have a small, round kitchen table with 4 chairs in our family room—perfect for puzzles, food and games.

I love it when our whole family is together during the Christmas holidays or other times, when we all spend time together doing puzzles, watching sports and relating with each other.

## RELATIONSHIPS

The family room is about our relationships. Relationship and communication is extremely important to God. It was His desire to be in a special relationship with Adam and Eve, so He made them different from every other being He created. He made them in His image.

We can look through the Bible for this theme of

relationships and see that God has always reached out to have relationship with the people He created.

God revealed himself to Abram, seeking a relationship with him, and was delighted with Abram's faith. So much so, God changed his name and made him promises that are still in effect to this day, 4000 years later.

He revealed himself to Moses and raised him up as a deliverer to rescue His people from slavery. Moses would meet with God and the glory of the Lord would come on him so that he would literally shine with the glory of the Lord. So much so, that Moses took to putting a veil on his face, so the people would not see the glory fade. When Miriam and Aaron opposed Moses this is what the Lord said to them,

Numbers 12:8

> With him I speak face to face, clearly and not in riddles; he sees the form of the Lord. Why then were you not afraid to speak against my servant Moses?"

Clearly, God had an intimate relationship with Moses!

We could talk about so many of the saints of old; Samuel, Elijah, Jeremiah, Daniel, David—the shepherd boy who worshipped God when no one but the sheep and the Lord were watching, David—the teenager who took on and took down the giant who was taunting the armies of Israel. But David did not see it that way. Goliath was not just taunting the armies of Israel, but the armies of the Living God.

David was known as a man after God's own heart. God loved him so much that when David wanted to build a house for Him, the temple (they were still worshipping God in the tabernacle in David's time), God told him, "No. David, you will not build a house for Me. But I will build a house for you." And Jesus comes from the line of David. How God honours those He loves!

I love that the love of God is so great. The Scripture, found in John 3:16-17, is one of the great revealers of the heart of God.

> 16 For God so loved the world that he gave his one and only Son, that whoever believes in him shall not perish but have eternal life.
>
> 17 For God did not send his Son into the world to condemn the world, but to save the world through him.

## GOD IS A FATHER

Jesus introduced God in a way that was not common, and practically unheard of among the rabbis in His day. He called God, "Father." When Jesus prayed, He addressed God as Father; when he taught, He referred to God as Father—His Father and our Father! It was a key part of His message.

And God had confirmed that relationship publicly at Jesus' baptism, when the words thundered from heaven, "This is My Son, in whom I am well pleased."

This was a new understanding. Sure, there are a few verses in the Old Testament that refer to the concept, but the emphasis Jesus put on it got him into some deep trouble with the Teachers of the Law; the scribes and Pharisees.

Jesus was revealing the Father-heart of God. Jesus was introducing us to relationship with God. Not only is God the King, Creator and all the other things He revealed Himself to be in the Scriptures; but He is our Father.

This was radical in His time. God is a family man—er, ummm a Family God!??

He calls us, "sons," and "daughters;" and, unlike all earthly fathers, He is perfect as a Dad.

We are told that He is our Abba, our Daddy.

Galatians 4:6

> Because you are his sons, God sent the Spirit of his Son into our hearts, the Spirit who calls out, "Abba, Father."

It follows that, if God is our Father, we are family with other believers and, in a sense, with everyone. In fact, the New Testament Scriptures refer to us as, "brothers and sisters."

When I was growing up, my sisters, brother and I would, on occasion, ask our mother what she wanted for Christmas or for her birthday. Her answer was always the same, "Good children."

We must have been little terrors! At times, we certainly were! But, is it not the desire of every parent to have good children, to have peace and unity in the home?

God is no different. We are exhorted to love one another.

1 John 4:21

> And he has given us this command: Anyone who loves God must also love their brother and sister.

He wants us to live in harmony with each other.

Romans 12:18

> If it is possible, as far as it depends on you, live at peace with everyone.

He wants us to put forth some effort toward reconciliation, if needed.

Matthew 5:23

> 23 "Therefore, if you are offering your gift at the altar and there remember that your brother or sister has something against you, 24 leave your gift there in front of the altar. First go and be reconciled to them; then come and offer your gift.

We are to put others first, laying down our lives for them.

1 John 3:16

> This is how we know what love is: Jesus Christ laid down his life for us. And we ought to lay down our lives for our brothers and sisters.

We are to be patient, humble and gentle with others.

Ephesians 4:2

> Be completely humble and gentle; be patient, bearing

with one another in love.

We are to forgive each other.

Colossians 3:13

> Bear with each other and forgive one another if any of you has a grievance against someone. Forgive as the Lord forgave you.

Ephesians 4:32

> Be kind and compassionate to one another, forgiving each other, just as in Christ God forgave you.

## FORGIVENESS IS A CHOICE

Forgiveness is the heart of the gospel. God forgave us, so we also should forgive each other.

Unforgiveness is a huge burden to carry. It locks us to people and situations in unhealthy ways; ways that keep us tied to them, ways that ultimately create a poison in us that becomes detrimental to our emotions, relationships, ability to cope, health… It just isn't good. Unforgiveness can create a bitter root in us that will ultimately destroy us.

Hebrews 12:15 tells us:

> See to it that no one falls short of the grace of God and that no bitter root grows up to cause trouble and defile many.

The bitter root causes trouble and defiles many. The other place in Scripture where it mentions a bitter root is in Deuteronomy 29:18

> 18 Make sure there is no man or woman, clan or tribe among you today whose heart turns away from the Lord our God to go and worship the gods of those nations; make sure there is no root among you that produces such bitter poison.
>
> 19 When such a person hears the words of this oath and they invoke a blessing on themselves, thinking, "I will be safe, even though I persist in going my own way," they will bring disaster on the watered land as well as the dry.

Verse 18, speaks of worshiping other gods, not our God, and that is referred to as a root that produces bitter poison. The following verse, 19, deals with believing a lie, that we will be safe even when we persist on going our own way. Oh, that we would want to walk the way God has for us and not persist in going our own way!

Let's get back to our previous thought—on forgiveness—in light of these verses. Forgiveness is God's way. Holding on to the offense is not His way. As the verse in Deuteronomy says, it will bring disaster on the watered land as well as the dry. It will cause our 'well' to dry up. Things will not be 'well' with us, and that 'well' within us—the Holy Spirit, will be quenched because we give the enemy place. By holding onto the offense and remaining in unforgiveness, we agree with the enemy's design for the person who wrongs us.

Matthew 18 is the "go to" chapter for forgiveness. That is where we find Jesus telling the story of the unmerciful servant. Do you remember the story?

> 21 Then Peter came to Jesus and asked, "Lord, how many times shall I forgive my brother or sister who sins against me? Up to seven times?"
>
> 22 Jesus answered, "I tell you, not seven times, but seventy-seven times.
>
> 23 "Therefore, the kingdom of heaven is like a king who wanted to settle accounts with his servants. 24 As he began the settlement, a man who owed him ten thousand bags of gold was brought to him. 25 Since he was not able to pay, the master ordered that he and his wife and his children and all that he had be sold to repay the debt.

26 "At this the servant fell on his knees before him. 'Be patient with me,' he begged, 'and I will pay back everything.' 27 The servant's master took pity on him, canceled the debt and let him go.

28 "But when that servant went out, he found one of his fellow servants who owed him a hundred silver coins. He grabbed him and began to choke him. 'Pay back what you owe me!' he demanded.

29 "His fellow servant fell to his knees and begged him, 'Be patient with me, and I will pay it back.'

30 "But he refused. Instead, he went off and had the man thrown into prison until he could pay the debt. 31 When the other servants saw what had happened, they were outraged and went and told their master everything that had happened.

32 "Then the master called the servant in. 'You wicked servant,' he said, 'I canceled all that debt of yours because you begged me to. 33 Shouldn't you have had mercy on your fellow servant just as I had on you?' 34 In anger his master handed him over to the jailers to be tortured, until he should pay back all he owed.

35 "This is how my heavenly Father will treat each of you unless you forgive your brother or sister from your heart."

Ouch! Ouch! Ouch!!! 'This is how my heavenly Father will treat each of you unless you forgive your brother or sister from your heart!'

How will they be treated?

He will hand him or her over to the jailers (some translations say tormentors) to be tortured until he should pay back all he owed.

There is no way to pay it back, is there? Our Father expects us to treat others with the same grace with which He has treated us.

We are locked up and tormented until we forgive. Oh, I can assure you that our Father is not being mean. He is being just. If you do not choose to partner with His grace and His mercy, you have chosen to partner with the opposite; offense, unforgiveness, revenge, hatred, anger…you put the word in. All these are from the enemy's camp. And if you choose to partner with the enemy, you will be tormented by the spirits that are in that camp. It's not rocket science.

We can be free! In the prayer that Jesus taught His disciples, one part says…'forgive us our debts (sins or trespasses) as we forgive those who sin against us.' Only we have the key to that jail. God will not get us out. We can open that door and be free if we forgive.

## THE "HOW TO"

Some say, "I can't forgive, I don't feel like I can forgive." Or, "When I have forgiven, I don't feel like I have, so I am a hypocrite.

I have been in enough situations in my life where I have chosen to forgive. My first steps are usually the same. I take it to the Father, and I tell him what I'm feeling.

"So and so did this. I am devastated," or, "I am angry," or, "I am hurt…I choose to forgive them." Of course, I am naming them before the Father. "I ask that my feelings will come in line with my declaration. I release them to you. They owe me nothing."

I have done this over and over; sometimes about the same situation, if the feelings arise that I feel the need to, again, declare to the Lord my forgiveness. It is a process. I speak the words and believe that feelings will eventually line up with my declaration. I trust that God will do His part and bring healing to my emotions as well.

One time in particular, I wanted to make sure there were no blockages in my relationship with the Father, so I was spending time before Him asking if I needed to forgive anyone. Three people and the situations from which I needed to release them came to mind. As I dealt with each one, the Holy Spirit then brought back a memory where I had done something similar to someone else. How humbling! I asked Him to forgive me for those as well. I don't even remember what they were now, but the lesson was profound. We hold things against others that we ourselves do. We are just blind to it.

## JESUS IN MY FAMILY ROOM

Oh, it is time to invite Jesus into our family room—our relationships. Grab a pen, get yourself comfortable, and let's see what He wants to reveal to us. Write down what you hear, see and sense in the *Write it Down* section.

# INVITATION:

Jesus, come into my family room—my relationships; my relationships with You and with others.

- Show me how You see my family room.

- Show me if I have unforgiveness against others.

- I want to walk in Your ways.

For any situation that come to mind—walk with Jesus through it. Choose to forgive.

- I choose to forgive _____ for _____.

- I release them to You. Change my heart. Let me see them like You do.

- What do You have to say to me about that situation?

- Where were You when that was happening to me?

- How do You see me?

## WRITE IT DOWN...

# Chapter 3 — The Family Room

# CHAPTER 3 — THE FAMILY ROOM

# Chapter 4

# THE KITCHEN

*Above all else, guard your heart for everything you do flows from it.*
*Proverbs 4:23*

Ah, the kitchen—the heart of the home. My grandmother, who was quite a creative lady, had a framed embroidery piece she had made, hanging in her kitchen. It said,

"No matter where I serve my guests, it seems they like my kitchen best!"

Grandma Ramseyer was an excellent cook and baker. It did not matter to me where she served us; kitchen, dining room, living room or sunporch; her food always tasted good. Just thinking of her brings back the memory of some of the things she made that were my favourites; coconut butter tarts, chocolate covered Rice Krispie cookies, coffee cake, her homemade black raspberry jelly, and her whipped mashed potatoes. Ah, the joys of visiting Grandma and partaking of the bounty of her kitchen!

One time, when my sister and I were at Grandma and Grandpa's home for holidays, Grandma gave me a mild scolding, as only a Grandma can do. She was concerned that I only wanted to eat her jelly and not the other good things she made for the rest of the meals. I must have really enjoyed the jelly, because I still think of her jams with fond memories to this day, well over 40 years later!

What memories do kitchens conjure up for you? Baking favourite desserts—or eating them? Loud bantering during meal times—or quiet reflective ones? Doing dishes by hand—or loading the dishwasher? We did have a dishwasher growing up, but not until I was well into my teen years! Before that, the dishwasher was usually my mother, with the dish dryers being my older sister and I. It seems like we always had to use the bathroom when it was time for dishes!

Yes, the kitchen is the heart of the home; where meals are prepared and eaten, where the family gathers, and where the children's homework gets done.

## THE HEART

In our world, when we talk of matters of the heart; we speak of love, of courage, of pride. I just read through 725 scriptures with references to the 'heart'. Did you know we can have an understanding heart or a fearful one? We can have hearts that are full of wisdom, integrity, generosity; hearts that hold secrets; hearts that are pure, blameless, steadfast, secure, upright, willing, peaceful, and discerning.

Conversely, our hearts can also be wounded, broken, stricken, faint, numb, trembling, discouraged, hard, obstinate, corrupted, unyielding, deluded, perverse, stubborn, adulterous, or divided.

We are not talking just about the heart—the organ that beats within us. It is certainly an integral and amazing part of our body. We are talking of something more than just our physical heart; something that goes to the core of who we are as a human being.

Do you know that you think with more than just your mind (head)? The Bible tells us that we also think and meditate with our hearts.

Psalm 19:14

> May these words of my mouth and this meditation of my heart be pleasing in your sight, LORD, my Rock and my Redeemer.

Matthew 9:4

> Knowing their thoughts, Jesus said, "Why do you entertain evil thoughts in your hearts?

I heard a captivating interview a number of years ago with Dr. Aiko Hormann. She was in her early 80's at the time of the interview and had been a Research Scientist in the 1960's for the Pentagon. She talked about how we have 3 brains—our head brain, heart brain and gut brain. Our hearts and gut have almost as many neurotransmitters as our brain, and memories are stored in these areas. I am not a scientist, but I did see that there are more articles on the internet about this concept. One article I read was entitled, "Your heart and stomach may be smarter than you think." I like that! So science is backing us up on what the Bible has been telling us.

We think with more than just the rational part of our head brain. We think with our heart and with our gut too. Have you ever been so disappointed you actually feel your stomach drop? Or so "nervous" that you have butterflies in your stomach? Your head brain may be telling you that there is no reason to be afraid but your stomach is telling you something else.

We really are fearfully and wonderfully made.

I would encourage you to check out some of Dr. Aiko Hormann's materials. She is a Christian and has used her research in conjunction with her understanding of Scripture to bring healing, transformation and freedom to many people.

## APPETITE

What are you hungry for?

If I go into the kitchen, I can open the fridge or cupboard and usually find something that will satisfy my hunger.

Sometimes, I may pick something healthy like some fruit or vegetables. Or I may decide I want a cookie, chocolate, cake, or something that will satisfy what my appetite is wanting, but is certainly not good for me!

The same is true when I am making meals. I can choose to make a healthy meal or a meal that is not healthy. Having athletes in the house has made me more aware of wholesome choices in meal preparation.

If I make healthy meals, my family and I are fueled well for the activities at hand, be that work, school, or other activities. If the meals I make are not healthy, it can negatively affect our performance in those same activities, as well as have negative effects on overall health and wellness.

The same is true in the spiritual. What appetite will we feed?

Paul warns the believers in Rome about persons who were causing divisions among the believers there because of their appetites.

Romans 16:18

> For such persons do not serve our Lord Christ, but their own appetites, and by smooth talk and flattery they deceive the hearts of the naive.

What does he say about those who were serving their own appetites?

I repeat Paul again for emphasis, "For such persons do not serve our Lord Jesus but their own appetites."

Our appetites can give our Father pleasure or heartache.

The Lord was pleased when Solomon asked for a discerning heart to govern His people and to distinguish from right and wrong. God not only gave him a wise and discerning heart, but also gave him what he did not ask for, that being, both riches and honour, so that in his lifetime there would be no equal among kings. You can read the account in 1 Kings 3:4-15.

In Genesis 6:6 we have the account of the Lord being grieved in His heart because of the sinfulness of man.

> And the Lord regretted that he had made man on the earth, and it grieved him to his heart.

We are made in the image of God. He has feelings too. And we can give Him pleasure and pain by our thoughts and actions.

One of the most horrible chapters in David's life starts off when he was not where he was supposed to be.

2 Samuel 11:1

> In the spring, at the time when kings go off to war, David sent Joab out with the king's men…But David remained in Jerusalem.

So starts the chapter of intrigue, infatuation, adultery, pregnancy, manipulation, murder, and concealment; and this by a man who was known to have a heart after God.

Jesus said in Mark 7:21

> 21 For it is from within, out of a person's heart, that evil thoughts come—sexual immorality, theft, murder, 22 adultery, greed, malice, deceit, lewdness, envy, slander, arrogance and folly.

## MASTERY

Way back, just after the garden, when Cain and Abel, the sons of Adam and Eve, brought sacrifices to the Lord—Abel's offering pleased God and Cain's did not. Cain was angry about it. Very angry, so much so, it affected his countenance.

And God spoke to him.

Genesis 4:6

> Then the Lord said to Cain, "Why are you angry? Why is your face downcast? If you do what is right, will you not be accepted? But if you do not do what is right, sin is crouching at your door; it desires to have you, but you must master it."

But Cain did not master it. He chose, instead, to partner with the sin that desired him and attacked and killed his brother. When the Lord asked him where his brother was, he lied and said he did not know, asking the Lord if he was his brother's keeper.

Wow, just a little aside here. It's never good to lie to the Lord. We may fool ourselves but never Him.

The Lord asked him, "What have you done? Listen! Your brother's blood cries out to Me from the ground. Now you are under a curse and driven from the ground which opened its mouth to receive the blood from your hand."

It keeps getting worse and worse. And that is the nature of sin. It brings a curse on you and your family. For the sins of the father are passed down 3 or 4 generations. (See Exodus 20:5, 34:7, Numbers 14:18, Deuteronomy 5:9)

David thought he would get away with his 'little indiscretion' with Bathsheba. No, it didn't work that way. She gets pregnant. Now he has to bring her husband home from the battle line so it will look like he is the father. And then Uriah, the husband, is too loyal, won't even go home to sleep with his wife, so David sends a message with Uriah when he heads back to the front. That message that Uriah carries, is his death sentence. It instructs the general to have the whole army pull back so Uriah is killed in battle. After the proper time of mourning David marries Bathsheba but the sin (and now sins) is not dealt with. They remain lying low to keep multiplying and bringing their sinister effects.

David is comfortable with his deceit. But the Lord is not pleased. He has to get the prophet Nathan involved. It is not until he is confronted, that David understands the magnitude of his sin, and its consequence. He is forgiven, but there are the consequences of his actions that he and his family will reap; the baby dies, David's oldest son, Ammon, rapes his half-sister, Tamar. Her brother, Absalom, later kills Ammon out of revenge, and eventually leads a revolt backed by Bathsheba's grandfather, one of David's trusted advisors, and takes the kingdom from David for a time.

Some of most beautiful Scripture comes out of that time when the prophet Nathan confronted David with the word of the Lord—

Psalm 51

> 1 Have mercy on me, O God,
>     according to your unfailing love;
>   according to your great compassion
>     blot out my transgressions.
>
> 2 Wash away all my iniquity
>     and cleanse me from my sin.

3 For I know my transgressions,
   and my sin is always before me.

4 Against you, you only, have I sinned
   and done what is evil in your sight;
so you are right in your verdict
   and justified when you judge.

5 Surely I was sinful at birth,
   sinful from the time my mother conceived me.
6 Yet you desired faithfulness even in the womb;
   you taught me wisdom in that secret place.

7 Cleanse me with hyssop, and I will be clean;
   wash me, and I will be whiter than snow.
8 Let me hear joy and gladness;
   let the bones you have crushed rejoice.
9 Hide your face from my sins
   and blot out all my iniquity.

10 Create in me a pure heart, O God,
   and renew a steadfast spirit within me.
11 Do not cast me from your presence
   or take your Holy Spirit from me.

12 Restore to me the joy of your salvation
   and grant me a willing spirit, to sustain me.

13 Then I will teach transgressors your ways,

> so that sinners will turn back to you.
> 14 Deliver me from the guilt of bloodshed, O God,
>    you who are God my Savior,
>    and my tongue will sing of your righteousness.
> 15 Open my lips, Lord,
>    and my mouth will declare your praise.
>
> 16 You do not delight in sacrifice, or I would bring it;
>    you do not take pleasure in burnt offerings.
> 17 My sacrifice, O God, is a broken spirit;
>    a broken and contrite heart
>    you, God, will not despise.

Through this time, David's heart is broken. He cries out for forgiveness and that he would be cleansed and made new.

In essence, he agreed with what the Lord had revealed. His sin was terrible, and he needed to confess and get his heart back on track. To do that, he was crying out to the only One who could really help in that department.

John 1:9 tells us

> If we confess our sins, he is faithful and just and will forgive us our sins and purify us from all unrighteousness.

We have a better covenant than David. Because of Jesus

death and resurrection, we are a new creation; we have Holy Spirit in us, not just with us, and we have the ability to break off the curse cycles and gain freedom.

But the principles are the same.

We have a choice. Will we partner with the sin that wants to master us? Or will we master it?

Romans 6:13-15

> 13 Do not offer any part of yourself to sin as an instrument of wickedness, but rather offer yourselves to God as those who have been brought from death to life; and offer every part of yourself to him as an instrument of righteousness.14 For sin shall no longer be your master, because you are not under the law, but under grace.

## ARE YOU HUNGRY?

There used to be a saying, "The way to a man's heart is through his stomach." The meaning was that, if a woman was good at making food, she would have no problem getting a husband.

I am not sure of the validity of that statement, but I do know that my husband loves food and thinks about it a whole lot more than I do.

In John 4:34 Jesus tells his disciples

> "My food," said Jesus, "is to do the will of him who sent me and to finish his work.

There is something vastly different between physical hunger and spiritual hunger. When you are hungry physically you will eat.

That is not necessarily the case spiritually. We may be hungry but we do not necessarily eat out of the right lunch box.

Jesus said in Matthew 5:6

> Blessed are those who hunger and thirst for righteousness, for they will be filled.

The children of Israel were fed supernaturally by the Lord for 40 years in the wilderness. This dew from Heaven rested; and, when it dried, it was what they called, "Manna"—"What is it?" It tasted like a wafer made with coriander seed and honey. Every morning but the Sabbath, it was out on the sand of the dessert; and they needed to go out and gather it.

God called it, 'Bread from Heaven'.

Jesus said in the Gospel of John, that He was the bread from Heaven. He said that, if we believed in Him, we needed to eat his flesh and drink his blood.

What was He saying? That our life is no longer our own—we are a part of Him, that his life flows into us; that He is in us, and we are in Him.

I have, at different seasons in my life, taken communion daily—just me and Jesus. I hold up the cup and the bread, and say, "Thank You for Your blood, shed for me. Thank you for Your body, broken for me. Thank You that You are in me and that I am in You.

Jesus wanted us to know that we were to be one with Him, even as He was one with the Father. Just as He was in the Father and the Father was in Him.

Same heart, same mind, same love…

## JESUS IN MY KITCHEN

It's time to invite Jesus in your kitchen. Get something to write with. Relax and invite Him to come. See what He wants to show you about your heart.

## INVITATION:

Jesus, come into my kitchen—my heart.

- Show me how You see me.

- What do I need to understand about my heart?

- What do You say about my appetites?

- Are there things that I need to let go?

- Teach me about mastery and how to overcome.

## WRITE IT DOWN...

# CHAPTER 4 — THE KITCHEN

# CHAPTER 4 — THE KITCHEN

# Chapter 5

# THE BEDROOM

> *For God speaks in one way,*
> *and in two, though man does not perceive it.*
> *In a dream, in a vision of the night,*
> *when deep sleep falls on men,*
> *while they slumber on their beds.*
> *Job 33:14-15*

The bedroom is the room in our home we probably spent the most time—sleeping!

When Paul and I were engaged, we went shopping to pick out our furniture for our first home together. I remember shopping for our bedroom furniture and mattress. I am rather picky, and I was looking for something particular for our bedroom set. I did not find exactly what I was looking for, which is often the case with me, but something close.

The mattress, too, was an interesting decision. There were a lot of options for mattresses, as water beds were very popular when we were married. We decided on a type of water bed that looked like a normal mattress and box spring set, but the mattress zipped open and had long plastic tubes that fit into the mattress and that were filled with water. It was during my third pregnancy, that I had finally had enough of that mattress—it had to go! Out it went for something more firm and helpful for my back.

The bedroom is the place for sleep, rest, dreaming, changing, and intimacy.

## SLEEP

How do you sleep? Are you the type that is asleep before your head hits the pillow? Or are you reflective, needing to go over every aspect of the day before you sleep?

I tend to lean towards the second category while my husband is the kind that can sleep anywhere, anytime; and he often does if he wants a short nap.

I have, at times, found sleeping difficult, as I am reflective, like to ponder, and am quite analytical. I can look at a scenario from multiple perspectives and dissect it, as well, as I lay in bed. Throw in my sensitivity, and it gets more complicated yet…and the traffic noise, especially when it's raining, the ceiling fan, with its unbalanced hum in the spring and summer, and the occasional snoring sounds that come from the other side of the bed. I am painting quite a picture of unrest and wakefulness in the night!

Thankfully, all my nights are not like that!

## WORRY AN ENEMY OF REST

Often, it is the things that are unresolved that want to dominate our minds when we want to sleep. It is the things that trouble and worry us that cause us issues. It is hard to relax when we are stressed over these things.

We are told over and over in Scripture to not worry and not to fret.

Psalm 37:8

> Refrain from anger and turn from wrath; do not fret—it leads only to evil.

Matthew 6:25-27, 33

> "Therefore I tell you, do not worry about your life, what you will eat or drink; or about your body, what you will wear. Is not life more than food, and the body more than clothes? Look at the birds of the air; they do not sow or reap or store away in barns, and yet your heavenly Father feeds them. Are you not much more valuable than they? Can any one of you by worrying add a single hour to your life? ...
>
> 33 But seek first his kingdom and his righteousness, and all these things will be given to you as well.

This Matthew 6 passage follows Jesus telling those listening that they cannot serve both God and money—it doesn't work to have two masters. Therefore…He transitions into the 'do not worry' passage.

You think you don't have enough money to live; enough for food, enough for clothes, enough for shelter. "Don't worry," says Jesus. "Your Father, who takes care of all the birds of the air, Your Father who clothes all the flowers of the field, will He not take care of you too? Seek first His kingdom; put Him first; and you will get all these things as well."

We learned earlier to take every thought captive to the obedience of Christ. This is the key to rest.

## PUTTING FEAR IN ITS PLACE

To sleep well, we need to put fear in its place.

Proverbs 3:24

> When you lie down, you will not be afraid; when you lie down, your sleep will be sweet.

The spirit of fear does not originate from God!

2 Timothy 1:7

> 7 For God has not given us a spirit of fear, but of power and of love and of a sound mind. NKJV

Haggai 2:5

> 'This is what I covenanted with you when you came out of Egypt. And my Spirit remains among you. Do not fear.'

What did a whole lot of angels have to say when they showed up to give messages to men and women?

"Do not fear."

Why? Because, we have a tendency to fear—fear of the unknown, fear of man, fear of failure, fear of not enough. What are your fears?

Do they keep you awake at night? Whether they keep you awake or not, it is time to change the way we think.

Fear is a spirit. It is a spiritual reality that wants your agreement. When I am fearful, I try to get perspective on this. I have battled this thing for years. If I can picture this as a demon, which it is, then I can choose simply to break my agreement with it and ask for Heaven's perspective.

Quite a number of years ago, a friend of mine, Laura Gerber, had a vision that she shared with me. In it, she saw me; and, before me was a huge spirit of fear. The vision shifted, and she saw this spirit from another angle. It was like a mask, a facade, thin—not much substance to it. She saw Jesus behind me. He was much bigger than the demon. He blew fire through me and out of me, and the demon went up in flames. All that was left was its ashes; and I danced on them. Then, I was able to get a sword and cloak that had been on the other side of the demon. Her vision went on, but that is the part I want to share with you.

Fear will keep us from moving forward and accessing all that God has for us. Fear will keep us from our destiny.

Fear is a funny thing. It is a threshold—a doorway—

we must walk through. Every time I do, I wonder what it was that really kept me back; because once I had broken through, I realized that it was really nothing but an illusion that wanted to keep me from moving ahead.

Job said an interesting thing when he found himself in journey of loss and suffering. He said in Job 3:25

> For the thing I greatly feared has come upon me, And what I dreaded has happened to me.

What we agree with, can open the doors to the enemy. Do not let fear rule your life. Let peace come and reign in you and through you.

Psalm 4:8

> In peace I will lie down and sleep, for you alone, Lord, make me dwell in safety.

## PEACE AND REST

Rest is an important concept to God. He worked creating the heavens and the Earth for 6 days; and then, on the 7th day, He 'rested'.

He liked that concept so much that He instituted a law that the Israelites were to rest on the 7th day as well. Work 6 days; rest on the 7th.

When the children of Israel were to enter the Promised Land, He also called taking possession of the land their "rest." The author of the book of Hebrews goes into some depth about why a whole generation died in the wilderness and did not enter their rest—because of unbelief.

We want to position ourselves for peace, to position ourselves for rest. One way to do this is to release the negatives that war against our soul and our spirit; the worries, the cares can be given over to God.

1 Peter 5:6-8

> 6 Therefore humble yourselves under the mighty hand of God, that He may exalt you in due time, 7 casting all your care upon Him, for He cares for you. 8 Be sober, be vigilant; because your adversary the devil walks about like a roaring lion, seeking whom he may devour.  NKJV

I often will verbally give the Father my cares, my troubles, my worries. Then I thank him for the opposite: "Thank You that Your peace passes understanding; thank You that You supply all my needs; thank You for Your wisdom and understanding."

Research some Scriptures around what your issue is and use them to battle with thankfulness.

## DREAM

God wants to speak with us. That can happen in numerous ways. But, because we are speaking about bedrooms, we are going to explore the subject of God speaking to us through our dreams.

Firstly, it is Biblical. We have record of God speaking to multiple people through their dreams; Abraham, Abimelech, Jacob, Laban, Joseph, the butler and baker in the Egyptian prison, Pharoah, the warrior Gideon overheard, Solomon, Daniel, Nebuchadnezzar, Joseph (Mary's husband), and Pilate's wife.

These dreams foretold events, gave instruction, issued warnings, and communicated the heart of God. In Solomon's dream, he had a chat with the Lord.

We are told in Numbers 12:6 that God speaks to prophets in dreams.

> Then He said, "Hear now My words: If there is a prophet among you, I, the Lord, make Myself known to him in a vision; I speak to him in a dream."

Through the Prophet Joel, we are told that something greater is going to happen. The Spirit of God will be poured out on all flesh, and there will be prophesying and dreams and visions by sons and daughters and the aged. God will get His heart and thoughts communicated through His Spirit to all.

Joel 2:28

> "And it shall come to pass afterward That I will pour out My Spirit on all flesh; Your sons and your daughters shall prophesy, Your old men shall dream dreams, Your young men shall see visions."

Do you dream? Do you remember them?

Dreams often have symbolic language that can make them seem rather crazy. We know that, at times, dreams need to be interpreted. Joseph and Daniel both had the gift to interpret dreams.

Not all dreams are from God, but it is one of the ways He does speak. Pay attention to your dreams. Our Father might want to give you insight, issue a warning, reveal heart issues, call you to repent, have you intercede for someone, or show you what is coming.

I often have dreams at the changing of seasons in my life to give me understanding that there is significant shifting coming. I keep a notebook by my bed to write down dreams that I have and ask the Lord to give the interpretation. I would encourage you to do the same.

## INTIMACY – THE BRIDE AND THE BRIDEGROOM

In the New Testament, we are often given the imagery that marriage is a picture of Jesus and the church. He referred to Himself as the bridegroom. He is coming for a pure and spotless bride. Even in the Old Testament, God referred to that same picture. He had married Israel. He was her husband.

We are told there is a mystery in marriage, or, rather, the relationship between Jesus and the church is like a marriage; and there is a mystery in that.

Ephesians 5:25-33

> 25 Husbands, love your wives, just as Christ loved the church and gave himself up for her 26 to make her holy, cleansing her by the washing with water through the word, 27 and to present her to himself as a radiant church, without stain or wrinkle or any other blemish, but holy and blameless. 28 In this same way, husbands ought to love their wives as their own bodies. He who loves his wife loves himself. 29 After all, no one ever hated their own body, but they feed and care for their body, just as Christ does the church— 30 for we are members of his body. 31 "For this reason a man will leave his father and mother and be united to his wife, and the two will become one flesh."

> 32 This is a profound mystery—but I am talking about Christ and the church. 33 However, each one of you also must love his wife as he loves himself, and the wife must respect her husband.

God has some boundaries set up around marriage. Some laws of the land have changed around this, but we will look at what God in his Word says.

Marriage is a covenant between two people; male and female.

It is to be exclusive. Adultery was expressly forbidden. In the Law, there was a sentence of death that went with it.

Divorce, while permitted, 'was allowed because of the hardness of heart'. Jesus said that. He also pointed the listeners back to God's heart and original intent. 'That a man should leave his father and mother and be united with his wife. What God joined together men should not separate.'

As in the Ephesians passage, Jesus gave Himself up for the church—died for us, so that we could be made new, be transformed into all that we are destined to be.

Even as the children of Israel were to have no other gods and love and serve only the One True God, we are to do likewise.

Jesus is our bridegroom. We are to remain true to him.

## JESUS IN MY BEDROOM

It's time to invite Jesus into your bedroom. Get a pen to write with. Relax and invite Him to come and meet with you.

# INVITATION:

- Jesus, I invite You to come into my bedroom.

- Show me what this room looks like from Your perspective.

- Show me Your heart for me in my bedroom

- Tell me what I need to release to have peace and rest.

- Is there a dream that You have given me that You want to speak to me about?

- Would You give me an ability to remember the dreams You do give me and an ability to understand what You are showing me through them?

## WRITE IT DOWN...

## CHAPTER 5 — THE BEDROOM

# CHAPTER 5 — THE BEDROOM

# Chapter 6

# THE DEN

*To you it has been given to know the secrets of the kingdom of heaven, but to them it has not been given.*
*Matthew 13:1*

Do you have a den? Growing up, we had one in our basement. It was a panelled room that had an alcove for an entry, with two doors that housed large storage closets on each side of the deep doorway. Inside the room there was my father's large desk and a muted, greenish-yellow coloured patent leather-like sofa that could flip down for an extra bed. We liked to play in that room at times. Eventually it became my brother's bedroom, and then the den no longer existed.

Dens tend to be generally smaller rooms used for

private uses, be that studies, libraries, TV rooms, or for home computers. If you have a den, how do you use it?

Dens also can have connotations for illicit activities—things that are done in secret.

## SECRETS

Do you have secrets? Things no one knows except you, and which you don't want anyone to know. They could be of positive or negative nature.

When I was a girl, I had a secret imaginary friend. My sister was very jealous, because I would not introduce her to my friend. My friend would pop out the window whenever my sister would come in the room. At least that is how I remember the story.

Some secrets are just that—things we have no need to let others in on. Helping someone out with a need anonymously, or paying it forward for someone (blessing them with a coffee, or paying for their meal or something nice that blesses another person you do not know.) We don't have to tell the world about these things.

In fact, Jesus tells us that there are times that we are not to let our left hand know what are right is doing. This means that there are times that we don't want others to know about our good deeds because God sees it, and that is enough.

There is a story, in Acts 10, about a devout Roman Military Commander, named Cornelius. He was a Roman; not a Jew; and not a follower of Jesus. But he was a God-fearing man and had done much good for the people in his area by giving to people in need, and he prayed to God regularly.

Do you know that God is so pleased with people who have hearts like that? In fact, God was so pleased with Cornelius that, one day, Cornelius had a vision. In the vision, he distinctly saw an angel who called him by name. It freaked him out! He wondered what this was about. The angel told him that his gifts and offerings came up before God as a memorial offering. He was told to send for Simon Peter and where to find him.

God loved this man who had such a compassionate heart. His continual good deeds were noticed by God, so God let him know that He was pleased and wanted him to have understanding about Himself. God told him to send for Peter who would tell him about Jesus and the way to the Father. How beautiful!

In the meantime, God had also spoken to Peter through

a trance. God wanted to make sure that Peter would, indeed, go with Cornelius' men because Jews did not want to associate with Gentiles. God also wanted to break down that understanding and move the church into extending salvation to the nations.

God sees our secrets. Those things that are according to His kingdom heart, He will reward. When we are in opposition to His will, which means we are in agreement with His enemy, we position ourselves on the wrong side of things. In the end, it will not go well with us if we remain in that place.

## REFLECTION

When our secrets are of a negative nature, such as when we do something for which we are ashamed or don't want others to know about because of fear or embarrassment, unrest is created within us. Perhaps we have clearly crossed the line on something, but we feel vindicated because we wanted revenge, to lash out, or to get back at someone. There are many possibilities of what our secrets may be.

These negative secrets may or may not be sin, but they have unfavourable effects in our lives.

When our secrets are sins, Numbers 32:23 tells us:

> …and you may be sure that your sin will find you out.

And Hebrews 4:13 tells us

> Nothing in all creation is hidden from God's sight. Everything is uncovered and laid bare before the eyes of him to whom we must give account.

I think that if we need to give an account, we might as well start the discussion now because He is gracious and kind; and it is His kindness that leads us to repentance. (Romans 2:4)

## REPENT

There was a song we use to sing years ago. The words were:

"Well it's a new day. Think new thoughts. It's a new way. Change your heart. There's a new law in the land."

That sums up repentance. Change the way you think. Change the way you act.

Sometimes we get caught up believing that we have to "be sorry." Sorrow is okay—if it causes us to change the way we think and change the way we act; but if the root of sorrow is self-pity or self-preservation, and it does not cause us to make a change, then it is not effective.

When Jesus came, His message was, "The time has come. The Kingdom of God is near—it's within reach. Repent and believe the good news!" Then He went about demonstrating the kingdom—healing the sick, casting out demons, and raising the dead.

The same is true today. The Kingdom of God is near—it's within reach. It's right here. Repent—change the way you think; change the way you act. Let your thoughts come into line your Father's thoughts. Let what you do come out of that relationship and believe the good news!

## SHAKE OFF THE DOLDRUMS

Sometimes, especially if we have been a believer for a time, we can think that we have it all together. We understand the message of the gospel, and things become routine. Our edge becomes a bit dull, so to speak.

Worse yet, we can become set in our ways, thinking that we don't need to learn a whole lot more so that we close off our hearts to receiving the new things God wants to show us. We need to be a wary of this condition.

Jesus addressed some of these conditions to the churches of Asia Minor in the encounter that the Apostle John had with Him that was recorded in the Book of Revelation.

To the church of Laodicea, He said,

Revelation 3:16-18

> 16 So, because you are lukewarm—neither hot nor cold—I am about to spit you out of my mouth.
>
> 17 You say, 'I am rich; I have acquired wealth and do not need a thing.' But you do not realize that you are wretched, pitiful, poor, blind and naked.
>
> 18 I counsel you to buy from me gold refined in the fire, so you can become rich; and white clothes to wear, so you can cover your shameful nakedness; and salve to put on your eyes, so you can see.

Jesus doesn't like lukewarm. Hot or cold, People, hot or cold—He can't stomach lukewarm. Yuck!!!

Jesus said to the Pharisees, in John 5:39-40

> 39 You study the Scriptures diligently because you think that in them you have eternal life. These are the very Scriptures that testify about me, 40 yet you refuse

to come to me to have life.

Jesus wanted them to understand something. The Scripture will not save you. Your interpretation of Scripture will not save you.

John 17:3

> Now this is eternal life: that they know you, the only true God, and Jesus Christ, whom you have sent.

There is it—knowing the Father and knowing Jesus—relationship. That's salvation!

As it is in any relationship, we get to know Him better by spending time with Him.

## GOD HAS SECRETS

It is in this relationship with God, that He has some things to share with us. He has some secrets!

There are some things you will never know about me unless you have a close relationship with me. The same is true with God.

You may have heard that I make great a great chicken dressing casserole or delicious cinnamon buns. You might even believe that the report is true; but unless you come over to my house and eat what I prepared, you would have only heard about it and not experienced it for yourself.

The same is true with God. There are things that only make sense when experienced. I may know in my head that He loves me but unless I have experienced His love, I do not really know it.

Even the followers of Jesus proclaimed what they had seen and heard—what they had experienced.

Acts 4:20

> As for us, we cannot help speaking about what we have seen and heard.

When we experience Him, He makes Himself known. He does have some secrets; and, just as you only tell secrets to your closest friends, so it is with him.

Get close enough to hear His heart. Get close enough to allow His secrets to change the way you view him, yourself and others. What He reveals to us becomes ours; we can own the revelation. We can own the promise. The things revealed to us become ours; and, not just ours; they become the inheritance of our children and our descendants forever.

Deuteronomy 29:29

> The secret things belong to the LORD our God, but the things revealed belong to us and to our children forever…

## JESUS IN MY DEN

It's time to invite Jesus in your den. Get your pen and make room for Him to come.

### INVITATION:

- Jesus, I invite you to come into my den.
- Show me what this room looks like from Your perspective.
- Show me Your heart for me in my den
- What do You have to say to me about my secrets?
- What secrets do You want to share with me?

# WRITE IT DOWN...

# CHAPTER 6 — THE DEN

# CHAPTER 6 — THE DEN

# Chapter 7

# THE HOME OFFICE

*Now he who supplies seed to the sower and bread for food will also supply and increase your store of seed and will enlarge the harvest of your righteousness.*
*2 Corinthians 9:10*

The home office is "Business Central" in the home. That's where you will find the desk, computer, bills to be paid, and the bookkeeping records. Do you have a home office? Or is that function integrated in your kitchen, dining room, family room, or bedroom?

Our office is the room above the garage. When we moved in, I thought we would call it the library as we have quite a collection of books. We have bookshelves lining two walls of the room, and they are very full. But, no; calling it the library never stuck; it has been referred to as, "The Office," to this day.

I have probably spent more hours in that room than in any other room in the house, (except, perhaps, the bedroom). I have, at times, worked from home and have spent a great deal of time on the computer there.

Each household needs to determine how to run the house financially. There is income coming in from employment, investments, commissions, etc.; and there are bills to be paid; electricity, water, gas, phone, taxes, and insurance, to name a few. There are grocery and clothing needs, household cleaning supplies, and ongoing maintenance items. There are transportation costs; cars, maintenance, fuel, insurances, and bus passes. As well, there can be recreational pursuits; music lessons, sports, club memberships, and other expenses or investments on which you may be spending your money.

We always need more coming in than going out, so spending plans or budgets are good ideas to help run the household smoothly.

## STEWARDSHIP AND THE ART OF MANAGING

Jesus often told stories to help illustrate the Kingdom of God. In Matthew 25 Jesus tells the story about the master who went away and entrusted his wealth to his servants.

> 14 "Again, it will be like a man going on a journey, who called his servants and entrusted his wealth to them. 15 To one he gave five bags of gold, to another two bags, and to another one bag each according to his ability. Then he went on his journey. 16 The man who had received five bags of gold went at once and put his money to work and gained five bags more. 17 So also, the one with two bags of gold gained two more. 18 But the man who had received one bag went off, dug a hole in the ground and hid his master's money.
>
> 19 "After a long time the master of those servants returned and settled accounts with them. 20 The man who had received five bags of gold brought the other five. 'Master,' he said, 'you entrusted me with five bags of gold. See, I have gained five more.'
>
> 21 "His master replied, 'Well done, good and faithful

servant! You have been faithful with a few things; I will put you in charge of many things. Come and share your master's happiness!'

22 "The man with two bags of gold also came. 'Master,' he said, 'you entrusted me with two bags of gold; see, I have gained two more.'

23 "His master replied, 'Well done, good and faithful servant! You have been faithful with a few things; I will put you in charge of many things. Come and share your master's happiness!'

24 "Then the man who had received one bag of gold came. 'Master,' he said, 'I knew that you are a hard man, harvesting where you have not sown and gathering where you have not scattered seed. 25 So I was afraid and went out and hid your gold in the ground. See, here is what belongs to you.'

26 "His master replied, 'You wicked, lazy servant! So you knew that I harvest where I have not sown and gather where I have not scattered seed? 27 Well then, you should have put my money on deposit with the bankers, so that when I returned I would have received it back with interest.

28 "'So take the bag of gold from him and give it to the one who has ten bags. 29 For whoever has will be given

more, and they will have an abundance. Whoever does not have, even what they have will be taken from them. 30 And throw that worthless servant outside, into the darkness, where there will be weeping and gnashing of teeth.'

Firstly, let's note that the master was entrusting his wealth to these servants according to their ability. The first two doubled what was entrusted. The master was pleased, and they were promoted with more authority.

The third was afraid. He hid the investment and returned what had been given. He did not lose it, but it did not gain a return. The master was not pleased. It did not end well for that servant. The master called him 'worthless'. His actions did not bring any increase to the Kingdom.

## CALLED TO INCREASE

We are called to increase. Do you know it is even said of Jesus 'that He increased in favour with both God and man'?

Luke 2:52

> And Jesus increased in wisdom and stature, and in favor with God and men. NKJV

Increase is a theme throughout the Scriptures. It is first used in Gen 1:22 where God was pleased with the fish of the seas and birds of the air that He had made and declared that they should increase.

That is closely followed by the creation of man; male and female, in Gen. 1:28. He said that they were to increase in number, fill the Earth, and subdue it; that they should rule over the fish of the seas, birds of the air, and all the wildlife.

He spoke increase over Noah and his descendants after the flood as well as the creatures that had been on the ark. See Gen 8:17, 9:1, 9:7

He spoke increase over Hagar (Gen 16:10) that her descendants would be too numerous to count. He confirmed that to Abraham when He spoke of Ishmael's descendants in Gen. 17:20).

And He spoke increase to Abram, (Gen 17:1) in confirmation of His covenant.

He reaffirmed the promise that He had made to Abraham of increase to Isaac (Gen 26:24) and again to his son, Jacob, in Gen 35:10-12

10 God said to him, "Your name is Jacob, but you will no longer be called Jacob; your name will be Israel." So he named him Israel.

11 And God said to him, "I am God Almighty; be fruitful and increase in number. A nation and a community of nations will come from you, and kings will be among your descendants. 12 The land I gave to Abraham and Isaac I also give to you, and I will give this land to your descendants after you."

The Israelites increased greatly in Egypt; so much so, that they became a threat to Pharaoh.

They were given promises to increase in the land the Lord had promised to give them.

Deuteronomy 30:16

> For I command you today to love the Lord your God, to walk in obedience to him, and to keep his commands, decrees and laws; then you will live and increase, and the Lord your God will bless you in the land you are entering to possess.

He goes on to promise increase through His prophets. It was promised in material wealth as well.

Deuteronomy 8:17-18

> You may say to yourself, "My power and the strength of my hands have produced this wealth for me."

> But remember the Lord your God, for it is he who gives you the ability to produce wealth, and so confirms his covenant, which he swore to your ancestors, as it is today.

In this verse, we again see the word 'ability'. It is God who gives you the ability to produce wealth. As in the parable we read earlier, we are expected to do something with that ability.

We see increase in blatant, supernatural ways as well; in the story of Elijah and the widow with the supernatural provision of food. We see it in the story of Elisha with another widow, in the supernatural flow of oil that she could sell to pay off her debts. We see supernatural provision as Jesus turned water into wine at the wedding in Cana of Galilee as well as when Jesus fed, not only the multitude of 5000, but again in the miracle of the feeding of the 4000.

Jesus taught that the kingdom of God increases using terms like sowing seed, producing a harvest, or increase of investment.

## PERSPECTIVE

In the parable we read, the servant with the one bag of gold hid it out of fear. When having to give an account to the master, he said,

> 'I knew that you are a hard man, harvesting where you have not sown and gathering where you have not scattered seed. So I was afraid and went out and hid your gold in the ground. See, here is what belongs to you.'

What kept him from using his ability to create an increase?

It was his perspective. It was how he viewed the situation in which he found himself.

Firstly, he viewed the master as a hard man. He viewed him as one who prospered unfairly at another's expense. This created fear in him, so he did nothing with the investment, but kept it safe so it could be returned to the master. After all, his fear would rationalize that, if he lost the investment, it would not go well with him. The fear of being treated unfairly and the fear of failure were too much to overcome; he was too fearful to be able to step out and use his abilities to make a profit.

The master asked him why he would not have, at least, put it in the bank to gain interest? Why not? Perhaps he could not even trust the bank to keep this money safe?

Do you understand the heart of God for you that is wrapped up in this story?

How do you see your Father's heart towards you? Do you see Him as a stingy God, wanting to punish you at the first chance? Do you see Him as hard and interested only in your hard work for Him?

Or do you see Him as a Father who wants to give you opportunity to grow, expand, and make use of the abilities He has given you; abilities that can double what He has given, opportunities that will make room for more opportunities, promotions and authority in your life?

How you view the Father will either breed confidence or fear in you. A number of years ago, I was embarking on a new work adventure and was heading to a new supplier to make arrangements needed for a job I was working on. I was feeling anxious; and, as I was driving, the Lord spoke to me.

"Angie, do you believe that I am with you?"

"Yes," I replied.

"Well, act like it," He said.

I had to smile. I got it. He is with me; and, when He sends me on an assignment, He will equip me and give me what is needed; be that wisdom, understanding, favour—whatever is needed. However, I need to view the situation through the eyes of faith, not the eyes of fear.

Luke 17:5

> The apostles said to the Lord, "Increase our faith!"

We, like the apostles of old, need to ask the Lord to increase our faith as well. It takes faith to move ahead.

And without faith, it is impossible to please God. (Hebrews 11:6)

## EXERCISE YOUR FAITH MUSCLE

In Romans 12, Paul tells us to serve in proportion to our faith.

Romans 12:3-8

> 3 For by the grace given me I say to every one of you:

> Do not think of yourself more highly than you ought, but rather think of yourself with sober judgment, in accordance with the faith God has distributed to each of you. 4 For just as each of us has one body with many members, and these members do not all have the same function, 5 so in Christ we, though many, form one body, and each member belongs to all the others. 6 We have different gifts, according to the grace given to each of us. If your gift is prophesying, then prophesy in accordance with your faith; 7 if it is serving, then serve; if it is teaching, then teach; 8 if it is to encourage, then give encouragement; if it is giving, then give generously; if it is to lead, do it diligently; if it is to show mercy, do it cheerfully.

We are to use our gifts and abilities according to our faith. If our faith is little, we are to use our gifts and abilities to that measure. If our faith is large, we are to use our gifts and abilities to that measure.

Do you understand that, if we use the little we have, we grow in our faith. That is the point behind the parable. The master was angry because there was no faith used to increase what was given. Do not let fear hold you back. Use what God has given you. Use it in proportion to your faith. When you do, you will grow in your ability.

Exercise your faith muscle.

The kingdom principle is that there is always more than enough. In Heaven, there is no lack.

Philippians 4:19

> And my God will meet all your needs according to the riches of his glory in Christ Jesus.

When the blind men cried out to Jesus, He asked them what they wanted. They replied that they wanted to see.

Matthew 9:29

> Then he touched their eyes and said, "According to your faith let it be done to you"

And their sight was restored (verse 30).

You are called to walk by faith.

## JESUS IN MY HOME OFFICE

It is time to invite Jesus into your office. Get something to write with. Relax.

## INVITATION:

Jesus, I invite You to come into my office.

- Show me what this room looks like from Your perspective.

- Show me Your heart for me in my office.

- Expand my understanding of Your Father's heart for me.

- What do You have to show to me about my abilities?

- What am I called to be and do, that I have not seen before?

- Show me what has held me back and how to overcome.

# WRITE IT DOWN...

# CHAPTER 7 — THE HOME OFFICE

# Chapter 8

# THE GARAGE

*A good man brings good things out of the good stored up in him, and an evil man brings evil things out of the evil stored up in him.*
*Matthew 12:35*

Do you have a garage? Some houses I've lived in have had them, and some have not. The house we built had a nice double sized garage with a covered hole to drop firewood, stairway and basement under it to store the firewood. The house we are in now has barely a single sized garage. In fact, my husband's uncle, who built houses in our city way back, told us a story about the garage on our house.

Apparently, the owner had got a new car—a big, long new car. Unfortunately for him, the car did not fit in the garage. Fortunately for us, he added about 5 feet onto the front of the garage, bringing it out the front of the house, beside the porch and put a little roof on the extension that fit nicely under the second story window above it. I think it really improved the overall look of the house with the stone and roof. Of course the square footage added to the garage.

## STORAGE

The garage has useful space for storing all sorts of things. Firstly, for our vehicles, be they cars, trucks, 4-wheelers, or, in our case, bicycles—lots and lots of bicycles. When you live with cyclists who need multiple bikes for varying disciplines, you end up with a lot of bikes! We have not been able to fit a car in our garage for quite a number of years because of the bikes.

The garage may have tools, be they garden tools, yard tools, power tools, or the normal screwdrivers, hammers, wrenches or other hand tools. Then there are the outdoor activity games and sports equipment, the beach things, the extra lawn umbrellas, lawn chairs, and snow brushes, snow shovels, and extra snow tires. You may have a wagon, like us, or wheelbarrow, rubber boots and umpteen other items that need someplace to be stored.

You may also have a workbench in your garage; a place to fix items that need fixing or at least have the hammer, screws, nails, clamps, and other tools, handy and organized, ready if needed elsewhere.

A lot of the things that are stored in the garage have purpose. They are meant for a task. There comes a time when they are needed; not necessarily everyday, but there are times and seasons when they are useful and needed.

When I think of the garage, I think of something that Jesus said; something that jumped out at me a number of years ago when I was reading my Bible.

Matthew 13:52

> He said to them, "Therefore every teacher of the law who has become a disciple in the kingdom of heaven is like the owner of a house who brings out of his storeroom new treasures as well as old."

## UNDERSTANDING

What was Jesus talking about?

Every teacher of the Law—this is someone well versed in the Scriptures who becomes a disciple of the

Kingdom of Heaven—someone who is following Jesus and learning His Kingdom perspective.

Like the owner of a house who brings out of his storeroom new treasures as well as old—what is stored up is released, things of value both new and old.

This speaks to me of understanding. When Jesus was talking with Nicodemus, a teacher of Law who had come to Him at night about the Kingdom of Heaven and being born again, being born from above, Jesus questioned him about his lack of understanding.

John 3:10

> "You are Israel's teacher," said Jesus, "and do you not understand these things?

There needs to be understanding that goes with our knowledge. It is like having the puzzle with all the pieces but needing to put them together. We may have the pieces, but until 'this' piece is connected to 'that' piece, we do not see the full picture.

Understanding is more than just knowing the facts and more than knowing the details. It is an ability to have insight and comprehension of a matter.

We are told in Isaiah 11:2 that there is a spirit of understanding,

> The Spirit of the Lord will rest on him— the Spirit of wisdom and of understanding, the Spirit of counsel and of might, the Spirit of the knowledge and fear of the Lord

## YOUR EXPERIENCES

As well as our understanding of the Scriptures, like a treasure, we also store up a wealth of experience as we go through life. We experience joys and sorrows and walk alongside those that do as well. There are times we need to comfort and encourage or to rebuke and discipline others. We are faced with troubles and trials, heartaches and disappointments, as well as times of refreshing, hope and the mountaintop experiences.

All these are stored up in us as well. These experiences make us who we are. We are forged in the process of life.

How we view ourselves in the midst of this process and how we view our Father is key in how much of his Kingdom is released through us.

What is stored up in you?

What are your experiences? How has your Father met you? Have you turned to Him in the rough times? Or have you blamed Him? Have you thanked Him for the blessings, the provisions, the good things that have come your way?

In 2 Tim 2:20-21 Paul tells Timothy that

> 20 In a large house there are articles not only of gold and silver, but also of wood and clay; some are for special purposes and some for common use.
> 21 Those who cleanse themselves from the latter will be instruments for special purposes, made holy, useful to the Master and prepared to do any good work.

Do you understand we have a part to play in how we are used by our Father? Each situation that comes our way is a door. It is the door for a closer relationship with Jesus or conversely a more distant one.

If we choose Him and come close, we become more useful and set apart for his special purposes.

## YOUR TESTIMONY

Those who walked with Jesus had stories to tell of what happened to them, what He did, how things changed. They had experiences with Him.

Those that walked with Jesus after His death and resurrection had stories to tell of what happened to them, what He did, and how things changed. They had experiences with Him.

Today, when we walk with Jesus, we have stories to tell of what has happened to us, what He has done, and how things changed.

We call this our 'testimony,' or giving testimony of what we have seen, heard, touched—experienced.

Our testimony is important. We are told in Revelation 12:11 how the believers overcame the devil.

> They triumphed over him by the blood of the Lamb and by the word of their testimony; they did not love their lives so much as to shrink from death.

There are 3 things here that enabled them to overcome. First was Jesus' blood—what He accomplished for us on the cross has given Him the authority and power needed to break every bondage.

Second, it was the word of their testimony—they partnered with Jesus to align themselves with His purpose. He was active in their lives. He did stuff—amazing stuff—in their lives.

Lastly, they did not love their lives so much that they were not willing to die for Him. These believers, those who had experienced and loved Him, were living for Him and, conversely, were ready to lay it all on the line for Him.

These three things gave them the power to overcome in very trying times.

There is also another verse in Revelation that is interesting to note:

John was undone by the angel who brought the revelation, and he fell at his feet to worship him. But he was told in Revelation 19:10,

> "Don't do it!
>
> I am a fellow servant with you and with your brothers who hold to the testimony of Jesus. Worship God!
>
> For the testimony of Jesus is the spirit of prophesy."

Whatever Jesus does in your life He will do again. When you share what He has done, you open the door for Him to do it again for someone else.

If He healed you, He wants to release that to others. If

He spoke to you, comforted you, set you free from an addiction, healed your heart, put you back together or whatever He did, He wants to do again.

That's why it is important to share what He has done for you. It raises the faith level and enables Him to do it again. In essence, it becomes a prophesy to be fulfilled in others' lives.

## GO

Do you remember the story of the feeding of the 5000? It started with one little boy's lunch. It was blessed, and we are told that it was multiplied in the disciples' hands. Take what you have been given and give it out. See how the Lord multiplies it in your hand.

And so it is with the garage. There are things that are stored up—resources that are meant to go beyond the garage. Just as you get in your car and drive to whatever your destination is; work, the store, school, or any number of other activities, so you are also called beyond your own house.

You have a message to share with others. So go and share it.

## JESUS IN MY GARAGE

It is time to invite Jesus into your garage. Get something to write with, relax and invite Him to come.

> # INVITATION:
>
> Jesus, I invite you to come into my garage.
>
> - Show me what this room looks like from Your perspective.
>
> - Show me your heart for me in my garage.
>
> - What do you want to show me about my experiences in life?
>
> - Remind me of Your goodness and where You have worked in my life?
>
> - How do You want me to share these things?

## **WRITE** IT DOWN...

# CHAPTER 8 — THE GARAGE

# CHAPTER 8 — THE GARAGE

# Chapter 9

# THE BATHROOM

*And we all, with unveiled face, beholding the glory of the Lord, are being transformed into the same image from one degree of glory to another. For this comes from the Lord who is the Spirit.*
*2 Corinthians 3:18*

How many hours do you think you have spent before the mirror in your bathroom in the last week? Month? Year?

There are a number of things we do in front of that mirror in the bathroom. Speaking as a woman, perhaps we do a few more things than our male counterparts. I'm not entirely sure about that, given that I have a son who currently has long hair that is often tied up in a man bun!

What takes place in front of the bathroom mirror?

Hair—combing, brushing, drying, curling, straightening—to name a few activities…

Eyebrows—plucking, waxing…

Eyelashes—curling, mascara…

Teeth—brushing, flossing…

Face—washing, cleansing, moisturizing, makeup…

And the list can go on.

Why do we do these rituals? One would suppose that we do them so that we look good, feel good about ourselves, and because we want to present ourselves as well cared for and as attractively as possible.

## PERCEPTION

How do you see yourself? When you look in that mirror, who is looking back at you?

Do you see someone that you wish was shorter or taller, thinner or healthier? Are there things you wish you could change?

What is your perception of you? What do you believe about yourself?

When a teacher of the Law questioned Jesus about what he needed to do to inherit eternal life, Jesus asked this man what the Law said. The man summed up the Law like this:

Luke 10:27

> He answered, "'Love the Lord your God with all your heart and with all your soul and with all your strength and with all your mind'; and, 'Love your neighbor as yourself.'"

Jesus told him that he had answered correctly, and what to do so that he would live. The man wanted to justify himself, so he asked who his neighbour was; and Jesus went to tell the story of the Good Samaritan.

I want us to look at this from a bit of a different perspective. The Law said that we are to love our neighbours as ourselves.

When you look in the mirror? Do you love the person you see?

How can we truly love our neighbour, if we do not love ourselves?

How can we even evaluate this?

When you look in the mirror, what is your self-talk? What are your feelings telling you?

Sometimes we do things, not because we love other people, but because we want other people to love us. Sometimes we do things for others because we cannot say, 'No'. We do not protect our own interests, our own time, our own health, because we have not been taught to set healthy boundaries or don't have an understanding that boundaries are important.

I think of what the flight attendants demonstrate in their pre-flight instructions. If the plane should have difficulties, put the air mask on yourself and then help those around you. If you put it on your child first, who will help you when you have passed out from lack of oxygen? No, put it on yourself first and then you will have the ability to help others.

## HOW DOES GOD SEE US?

I believe that our perception of ourselves changes when we have a glimpse of how the Father sees us.

Is that not the story of Gideon? (Judges 6-8) In the time of the judges in Israel, before any kings, the children of

Israel would serve the Lord and then fall away and serve the other gods of the nations around them. When they would serve the Lord, they would be blessed; but when they served other gods, they would be overrun by their enemies. In their oppression, the people would cry out to the Lord; and He would raise up a deliverer who would set them free from the dominion and control of the nation that had overcome them. They would then serve the Lord for a time while that deliverer ruled as a judge or ruler over the land. The judge would die; the people would go and serve other gods and then the cycle would continue over again.

So when the story of Gideon begins, he is in a winepress harvesting the grain. Why? Because the nation oppressing them would destroy their crops, and they had to do their activities in secret.

An angel showed up while Gideon was doing this and said, 'The Lord is with you Mighty Warrior.'

Now, Gideon didn't believe that he was a mighty warrior. He was hiding out from the enemy.

The angel came from heaven with a message for him. "Go in the strength you have and save Israel from Midian's hand. Am I not sending you?"

Gideon had a few words to say about that and the impossibility of it. Basically, he was saying, 'But I'm a nobody!'

He was encouraged some more, "I will be with you, and you will strike down all the Midianites together."

Gideon believed the Lord. He needed a bit of encouragement, but he kept moving forward—pulling down the idols at his father's house, calling together an army, sending most of them home, and defeating the enemy armies with only 300 men.

Take the time to read the story in the story in Judges 6 and 7. It is rather fascinating.

I want to say to you, when you hear from Heaven your perception of yourself changes. When you get in touch with your purpose, the gifts you have been given, and the call on your life—you change.

Early in the journey of ministry, my husband, Paul, and I had started a church. A couple of years into that process, we went to a church-planters equipping event, called 'School for Apostles.' I felt intimated by the others there. They seemed more knowledgeable, more respectable, more supported, more schooled, and more anointed than me. I was wondering what I was doing there. I felt so inadequate.

The Lord spoke to me when I was mulling over how I felt. He said, "Do not call inadequate what I call adequate. It is not you who does the work anyway; it is Me. Be obedient."

I have never forgotten that. He has spoken to me and shown me, with clarity, my call and my giftings. I do not always know what that precisely means in any set of specific circumstances, but I do know the general direction.

When I know what He has said, I begin to align myself with that reality—His reality.

If I choose to believe what God has said, then some of what I have believed about myself has to go.

## FLUSHING

How convenient it is in the age and place in which we live, to have a bathroom, or two or more, in our homes! Just a generation before me, as my parents were growing up, they would have to make trips to the outhouse to relieve themselves. I remember, with interest, when visiting my grandparents how they had a chair called a commode. It had a hole cut out of the seat, and a pot sat underneath the hole. This commode was not used anymore, as their house at that time had a bathroom; but it was used, I suppose in the winter and at nighttime, at their farm before they moved to town.

This experience was rather foreign to me, and certainly to my children. Once, we took a trip up north to visit my aunt and uncle at their cottage by Kirkland Lake, in Northern Ontario. At the time we took the trip, our children were quite young. My aunt and uncle were adding to their cottage, and the bathroom was not yet finished. But there was an outhouse—a two seater—what luxury! When I took my five year old daughter out to use the outhouse, I explained that this is how people in the olden days went to the washroom. She was not pleased.

"But Mommy, this is not the olden days anymore!" she replied.

In light of what the Father may show us; in light of how he sees us, we will have some "flushing" to do.

I Corinthians 5:7

> Get rid of the old yeast, so that you may be a new unleavened batch—as you really are. For Christ, our Passover lamb, has been sacrificed.

Did you know that, for the Feast of Unleavened Bread, held in conjunction with the Passover that the children of Israel celebrated, they were to clean out their homes of any yeast? The Passover was instituted the night before the Hebrews left Egypt and their life of slavery. They were commanded to do various things which were a foreshadowing of what Jesus has done for us, to free us from our sins.

So, from this verse, we understand that there are some things, when Jesus visits us in our bathroom, that we will want to flush away; the old ways of thinking, to make way for the new thoughts and understandings. I love the part of the verse that says—that you may be a new unleavened batch—as you really are.

As you really are!

The Father sees you in a certain way. He has made you a certain way. And you are to be free from the lies and wrong thinking that says you are something other than what He says.

Gideon would have thought he was a coward and would have nothing to offer the nation. God said differently. When Gideon believed it and started moving with it, he became what God already knew about him, that he was a Mighty Warrior!

## SHOWER

Jesus is in the business of setting people free and cleansing them from their sin. John the Baptist prophesied over him, "See the Lamb of God who takes away the sin of the world."

That was why he came; to die as a sacrifice for our sins. Because of Jesus' death and resurrection, we can be free from our sins.

If you have plaguing thoughts of sin, confess them and be free.

As 1 John 1:9 says

> If we confess our sins, he is faithful and just to forgive us our sins and to cleanse us from all unrighteousness.

1 Corinthians 6:10 tells of the sins to which the Corinthians had been in bondage and, then, in verse 11, how they had been cleansed from such things by Jesus and Holy Spirit

> 11 And such were some of you. But you were washed, you were sanctified, you were justified in the name of the Lord Jesus Christ and by the Spirit of our God.

Ephesians 5:26 tells us how Jesus has sanctified us as his bride,

> that he might sanctify her, having cleansed her by the washing of water with the word,

Before Jesus was crucified, He washed His disciples' feet. Peter was horrified! Jesus insisted that He must wash Peter's feet if he was to be a part of Him. So Peter relented. Yes, Jesus could wash his feet, but he should wash all of him as well.

No, Jesus said he didn't need to wash all of him; he was clean because of the word spoken to him; he just needed to have his feet washed.

Take this to heart. If you are walking with Jesus, you are clean. But sometimes you need to have your feet washed.

In Jesus' time, they walked everywhere. They wore sandals. Their feet got dirty. It was common to wash them when they arrived at their destination. The uncommon part in the story is that Jesus wanted to wash their feet. That would have been a task for a servant.

In this demonstration, Jesus is modeling for them

leadership at its finest—serving, loving, laying down His right to be served in order to minister to the needs of others.

## JESUS IN MY BATHROOM

It is time to invite Jesus into your bathroom. Get something to write with, relax and invite Him to come.

### INVITATION:

- Jesus, I invite You to come into my bathroom.

- Show me what this room looks like from Your perspective.

- Show me how You see me.

- What do I need to flush away?

- Thank You that You wash me clean.

## WRITE IT DOWN...

# CHAPTER 9 — THE BATHROOM

# CHAPTER 9 — THE BATHROOM

# CONCLUSION

We are at the end of our house tour. Jesus may want an invitation into other rooms in your house. My hope is that, as you have begun to cultivate times where you come and sit at His feet, it will continue.

In Luke 10, we have the story of Mary and Martha. Jesus came to their house. Martha had a servant-heart and wanted to make a great meal and serve Jesus. Her sister, Mary, preferred to sit at Jesus' feet and to hear what He was saying. It caused a bit of a ruckus in the home when Martha appealed to Jesus to send Mary to help her.

Jesus had an interesting response. "Martha, Martha, you are upset about many things, only one thing is needed. Mary has chosen the better part and it will not be taken from her."

So much for convention, expectations and duties—they did not seem important to Jesus. What was important was that Mary had chosen what was best, and she got to keep it.

The Lord spoke to me one time about Mary and Martha. He told me I would be both Mary and Martha, but He wondered how I would know what to do if I did not come and sit at His feet.

So the invitation remains. Open the door, your door to all your rooms; invite Him in; make room for Him, and you will grow just as He promised.

You will grow in your love for Him and others, in your understanding of His heart and desire for you and those around you, in wisdom and stature before Him and before men, and in your ability to hear his voice.

Continue to make room in all your rooms!

# MORE ABOUT
# ANGIE & PAUL WAGLER

Angie Wagler is an author, speaker, mentor, and coach. Having a love for creative pursuits, she has worked in the arts; interior decorating, photography, and graphic arts as well as in administration and bookkeeping.

Angie has a heart for seeing the Church arise and become all it is called to be. She has a prophetic anointing, is an avid worshipper, singer, songwriter, and an inspired teacher.

Angie and her husband, Paul, are the founders of Arise Now—a ministry to encourage and equip. They have been church planters and pastors, and have been involved in church in various forms, including traditional, cell, house churches, and leadership healing groups. They understand wilderness pruning and fine-tuning and have an understanding of walking through the painful process that pre-empts inheritance.

Happily married for almost 30 years, they make their home in Kitchener, Ontario, Canada. They have three grown children and one much-loved dog.

Paul and Angie would love to hear how this book has impacted you. You can contact them through their website: arisenow.ca or the Arise Now Facebook page.

# OTHER BOOKS AVAILABLE

## —BY ANGIE WAGLER

This book,  is also available as an e-book in the kindle format from Amazon.

Watch also for Volume 2 in the Transformation Series **The Wilderness Training Manual** a resource to bring freedom from the slavery mindset and to access the promises of God!

## ALSO CHECK OUT
# PAUL WAGLER`S
## LESSONS LEARNED SERIES OF BOOKS;

### Lessons Learned on the Seat of my Bus—Vol 1

available in both kindle and paperback versions on Amazon. You will want to read this book to find out this bus driver`s secrets to enjoying life no matter what happens!

### What others are saying...

Paul writes from such a unique perspective bringing insight and humor into everyday life. Buckle your seat belt and enjoy the ride in reading this treasure.
   —Brian Fleming,  Author - "Your Life Matters"

Oh, Paul - you have hit the nail on the head. This book is so much fun! I love "Where you are seated determines your perspective." Each of the sections starts off like a tasty appetizer - and ends up with a nourishing nugget of God's truth. I look forward to your "Seat of the Bicycle" Book.
   —Jane Huff,  Author - "An Intimate Look at the Armour of God"

I can't stop laughing from the stories in your book! I'm sitting here alone in the living room just laughing out loud! Good Job!
   —Judith Ann Martin,  Blogger, www.HeyJude45.com

## Lessons Learned on the Seat of my Bike—Volume 2

also available in both kindle and paperback versions on Amazon. You will want to read this gem to find out some of this mountain bikers secrets to help you successfully navigate your life`s course!

## What others are saying...

Paul Wagler has done it again! A dynamic follow-up to his first book, "Lessons Learned on the Seat of My Bus: Secrets to Enjoying Life No Matter What Happens!", you'll enjoy how Paul delivers life changing lessons for avid cyclists, non-riders, mountain bikers, fair-weather riders, and everyone else in between. Ride along with Paul as he authentically shares the joys, the pains, the victories, and the mistakes he has experienced— on and off these non-motorized two wheels—so that you can gain gold nuggets about living a life that matters, pressing on, and finishing well. You'll even discover why you don't want a DNF or a DNS beside your name. Enlightening, practical and thought-provoking, well worth the read.

   —Jackie Morey, COO of Customer Strategy Academy; www.Your21stCenturyBusinessCard.com, www.CustomerStrategyAcademy.com, www.Your90DayLaunchpad.com

Paul's life can serve as an example for all of us. His use of stories from his biking experiences, to illustrate simple yet deep truths, is outstanding. He takes the complex and makes it simple. His book is a must read.

   —David Powers, Author and Coach; www.fear-to-faith.com

I enjoyed reading Paul's book. He has biking illustrations that fit pretty much all of life! And they are great illustrations! I feel myself limping as he runs with his bike shoes to the finish line! It's amazing!!

   —Jim Loepp Thiessen, Pastor

# ONE LAST THING...

If you enjoyed this book and found it helpful we would love if you would post a short review on Amazon. Thanks!

Made in the USA
Charleston, SC
21 March 2016